ON THE SPINE OF
ITALY

A Year in the Abruzzi

ON THE SPINE OF
ITALY

A Year in the Abruzzi

HARRY
CLIFTON

MACMILLAN

First published 1999 by Macmillan

an imprint of Macmillan Publishers Ltd
25 Eccleston Place, London SW1W 9NF
Basingstoke and Oxford

Associated companies throughout the world

ISBN 0 333 74619 8

1 3 5 7 9 8 6 4 2

A CIP catalogue record for this book is available from
the British Library.

Typeset by SetSystems Ltd, Saffron Walden, Essex
Printed and bound in Great Britain by
Mackays of Chatham plc, Chatham, Kent

To Deirdre

The greatest poverty is not to live in a physical world

WALLACE STEVENS

1 AT THE HEIGHT OF SUMMER, my wife and I moved unnoticed into a village in the Abruzzo mountains and began living there. Unnoticed, because although the village had a normal population of about ninety, the return of emigrants from America had swollen it to three hundred for the season. Throughout July and August, we were lost in the flux of coming and going, as temporary as the rest. Our only strangeness in the eyes of the village was that we spoke little Italian and no mountain dialect. We were the first outsiders to have stayed there.

All this mattered little at the time. It had to do with social relations – and the social relations between the villagers and their relatives home for the summer were conducted like public shouting matches, far into the small hours. They had each other to shout at, so why bother about strangers? Besides, social relations mattered little to us. We had come up there to be alone together and to write. Even if we hadn't, the midsummer heat would have kept us indoors, except for early morning and the hours after dark. The important thing was the house itself. Here, we had come into a strange and wonderful inheritance.

Our village was built around a square. In the centre of the square a mountain pine had been planted in what had once been the central well for drawing water. In the shade of the pine sat the old women, dressed in black. The parish church gave on to this little square. At its rear, through the sacristy,

1

a door connected it to an abandoned house, once the home of the parish priest when it was still worthwhile for the diocese to keep a priest in so tiny, high and remote a village. It was in this house we were living.

Not that we had just walked into it and taken up residence. A priest who worked in Teramo, the provincial capital, and who came up once a week to say Mass, allowed us the use of it. We could live there for nothing, he said, if we could bear the frugality and pay for our own food. That was in July, and the weather in the mountains would stay warm until September. Although neither he nor we knew it at the time, this was to be our home for a whole year.

We had seen it from miles away, a red sandstone house hard by the back of the church, as we toiled up the hairpin bends through the mountains. It stood across from us, clear in the evening light, but separated by a thousand-foot gorge around which we had to drive for a further fifteen minutes. Behind it and the village in which it stood, were the passes of the Gran Sasso, the highest peak in the Apennines.

The village, when we arrived that first evening, was silent, deserted. All over Italy, it was the dinner hour. In front of the houses, signs warned of dangerous dogs. Behind the signs, innocuous mutts slept unconcernedly. In the warm desertion of early evening, cats intrigued in the square. The sun was going down behind the mountains, reddening the stone of the houses. The sandstone of the parish house, which had been absorbing heat all day, was hot to the touch.

Inside, however, all was dark and cool. The windows were small, the stone walls two feet thick. The floor, where it was not bare stone, was cold terrazzo. The terrazzo was in what had once passed for a parlour, a room full of tasteless furniture and religious knick-knacks. A kerosene stove stood on four bandy legs against one wall, and pushed its crooked pipe through a hole in the ceiling. It was hard to imagine anyone had ever relaxed in so cold a room as this, an attempt at gentility, hopelessly out of place.

The last parish priest had been a man named Padre Simone. He had left a few years previously. He was working in another part of the mountains, not far away as the crow flies. He had worked in the tropics most of his life. In his old age, he had been given a quiet mountain parish. This, said our priest, was where the elder clergy were sent to live out their last years. He himself only came up to say Mass on Sundays and keep a minimal church presence in the village. The way he referred to it in passing, you could tell he had unspoken reservations.

'If you have any difficulty,' he said apropos of nothing, 'call me in Teramo. I'll bring you supplies on Sundays.'

In the kitchen, great hooks hung from the ceiling. There were still a few strings of dried vegetables hanging from them, from when Padre Simone had lived here. He lived like a bear in a cave, the priest said. The village women used to come in and clean up after him. On the wall, above a wooden table spread with oilcloth, an icepick hung. A sprig of ancient herbs gave the room a dry, spicy, lived-in air. In the blackened hearth, an iron pot was suspended. There, Padre Simone had cooked his meat. Unlike the parlour, here you could tell how time had passed for him, how he had been miserable and happy, alone with the ashes of his own fires.

These and a tiny bathroom were the only downstairs rooms. Under the flight of stone stairs was a clutter of unused religious objects – gilt statues of the Madonna and various saints, rusty chasubles hanging from meathooks by their own chains. We had taken up residence in the junk-room of a dying liturgy.

There were three rooms upstairs. Two were unused, with piles of old mattresses for the groups who bivouacked here on mountaineering trips. The third, which our Teramo priest had whitewashed and made habitable, was our bedroom. Its windows looked over the road to what had once been a schoolhouse. Now, the children were bussed to a neighbouring village, and the school had become a bar. Beyond the bar, north as far as the eye could see, were the brown peaks of the Apennines, the vertebral column of Italy, tortured by earthquakes and landslides. Our house, as we looked out from upstairs, seemed to drop away sheer into forested ravines, spaces to the north and east, the central point of which was the high, flat crown of Monte Gorzano.

'From Monte Gorzano,' our priest said, 'you can tell what weather is on its way here.'

It was an abandoned house we had moved into, drifted with light-motes and summer dust, and the hightide flotsam of religion on the ebb. But there was light and silence, space for the spirit to breathe. The ghosts were benign.

We heard a pounding at the front door. Gegeto, the village handyman and unofficial sacristan. He lived in the house above ours; the twisted fig tree in his garden threw green leafy shadows on our kitchen wall. He was a widower whose son was mayor of Poggio, a village two miles above ours and the administrative centre of the district. The mayor swept into our village once a week in his large car, to visit his father, drink in the bar and cast an eye over local affairs.

Gegeto lived alone, washed his own clothes, chopped fire-wood and cultivated his vegetable garden, as well as keeping the village functioning. That he liked us from the start was an important factor in our survival up there later in the year.

'He reckons you're going to be quiet.' The priest smiled. 'Others who have stayed in this house have played loud music constantly. He hates that – don't you, Gegeto?'

Someone else knocked, discreetly entered: Stefania, the official sacristan, in charge of candles and flowers, vestments and church linen. Both these people had rights of passage through into the sacristy, so the priest made a point of explaining the situation to them and to us. Gegeto adjourned to the bar, and with Stefania we crossed the square, which by now was getting dark and filling with the shouts of teenagers out playing and flirting in the hot night. Some greeted the priest dryly, others deliberately ignored him.

'The situation in this village is complicated,' he said. 'Some day I'll explain it to you.'

Stefania lived with her husband in a two-roomed house on the square. In summer it was an oven, but the houses, in their compactness, were designed for retention of heat in winter rather than coolness in the short, scorching summers. We sat in the downstairs room and drank coffee served on an inlaid tray. The giant television screen that dominated the room – it had an ultraviolet filter – flickered in front of us and killed off conversation. In the room above us, Stefania's husband was in bed, watching another television. Priests came and went, to be met with the ritual of coffee. For the monotony of village life though, there was no more complete antidote than the fantasy world of Italian television.

'An interesting woman,' the priest said, as we crossed again to the house. 'You will get to know her better as time goes by.'

The dinner hour was over. Cars, some elegant, others caked with dirt, were parked outside the bar. Out front, groups of men were playing card games, shouting numbers as they dashed their cards on to the tables. Children ran around screaming at the tops of their lungs, to approving glances from their parents. Behind the bar, a woman in catering uniform greeted the priest with measured politeness. She was serving scoops of ice-cream which everyone, from the hardened drinkers to the tiniest tots, was eating with equal enthusiasm. Ice-cream, greetings, the sound of children's voices – had we stayed a week, our impressions of the village would have come to no more than this.

The priest said goodbye, and drove back down to Teramo. On Sunday, he would be up again, with the provisions. Now it was Tuesday, and we had been travelling since the previous Sunday – through Rome, through the mountains to Ancona, down the Adriatic coast to Giulianova and inland through the shimmering heat to Teramo, where the priest had met us. We lay awake in bed, hearing a crescendo of argumentation and laughter across the road, dying away to isolated shouts in the small hours, and the huge silence of the mountains.

2 IN THE DAYS AND WEEKS that followed, we entered the rhythm of the village. In Italy, the functional side of life is addressed as early as possible in the day – the shopping, the housecleaning, the remunerative activities. The rest of the day is devoted to what really matters – dining in or out, socializing with friends and family, in private or in public. It is a rhythm peculiarly of the south. Climate and economics lend themselves to it. In the village, we saw it in microcosm.

At half past six in the morning, the bar across the road opened. The young woman whose turn it was to take the early shift, cleaned up after the night before and brewed the bitter black coffee the civil servants drank standing up at the bar before driving down for a morning's penpushing in the state offices in Teramo. Even here, where the men were either unemployed or doing seasonal work on the tunnel construction site in the mountains, a few had state jobs. These were little more than a form of social welfare, a token shuffling of papers on desks until one o'clock, then a return to the mountains to eat and begin their real day. After they had gone, there was silence again, broken only by the sound of the young woman sweeping the veranda in front of the bar, as light increased through the mountains.

On the ceiling of our bedroom, a streak of very strong light projected itself through an opening in the shutters. They acted like the shutters of a camera. We could see on the ceiling, elongated, upside down, the moving images of villagers passing in front of the house, until the photographic effect was broken by one of them pounding on our front door, with a letter or a box of fresh vegetables. The real day, our real day, had begun.

Someone was siphoning off water from the parish house. As we lay there, we heard it rushing through the pipe from the tank in the attic above us. It was left on for days and nights on end, but always disconnected when the priest drove in on Sundays. We traced the hosepipe under the road into a vegetable patch and horse pasture on a terrace below the village. There, it brimmed over in a rusty oildrum and seeped into the ground. With the noise from the bar at one end of the night and the noise from the water at the other, our candle burned at both ends in the summer months. But water was too old and complex an issue for blow-ins like ourselves to make a fuss about.

At this time, there was no shop in the village. Twice a week, at eleven in the morning, a travelling grocery driven by a man named Mario arrived. To get to our village from the neighbouring one, he had to describe a huge loop upvalley around the ravine. The road, seamed and patched from earth tremors and winter weathering, had taken sixteen years of work, strikes and politicking to complete its five kilometres of tortuous bends. It was the only way into the village, as the link on the other side with the mountain road to Poggio broke off at a collapsed bridge. Mario reminded the old village women of this, as they shouted in protest at his outrageous prices.

Loud, bald and muscular, in Hawaiian beach shorts, he looked like Benito Mussolini. His whippet-like wife, careworn from work and childbearing, her hair lank and unwashed, was the shadow side of the joy, the vitality. At forty-five she was expecting their seventh child. The other six had been left below in Teramo, while the pair of them worked the mountain villages all summer, their tinkling musical theme announcing them from afar. Their entrance to the village on hot blue mornings when we were upstairs at work was regal, deafeningly cheerful, interrupting everything. If we were slow in coming to buy, one of the old women was sent to pound on our door and remind us.

Not that we were ever short of food. Often a box of herbs, potatoes or carrots was left outside the door, or a crock of wild strawberries on the windowsill. It was summer, the season of abundance in the mountains, and the overflow came our way. When times got leaner later in the year, it would be a different story.

I moved into the end room, smelling of stone and the dust rising from junked mattresses and bedsteads. I set up a table by a window overlooking the ravine, and let myself be infiltrated by the sounds and smells, the tangible essences of the village. In that upstairs room of an abandoned house, through the long hot lulls of morning and afternoon, I worked with the shutters closed and the sun beating down outside, through the blinding weeks of July and August. Instead of displacement I felt, under that strange roof, only a sense of homecoming, a homecoming to the physical world.

> White walls, green shutters,
> Crusted loaves, that smelled of yeast
> From the travelling kitchens;
> Yellow plums, the fur of peaches

To the hand, ambivalent bells
At funerals and feasts –
All that was tangible, tasted, felt,
Restored us to our senses
Like freezing mountain water
From the spigots, or dialect
Stripped of abstraction, responses
Below language, blurred
And guttural, connecting
Things with their own word.

Outside, far to the north, stood Monte Gorzano. Long after our side of the mountains was in shadow, a blast of westering sun yellowed its upper slopes. We were in a closed valley. As evening deepened, it was like being in the belly of an interstellar telescope. There was only one way to look – upwards, into the blue of outer space. The Plough tracked its way round the peaks, in a giant annual circle. Late summer meteors raced along the stratosphere and burned out.

On those fine summer evenings, we went out walking with Stefania, on the forested road that stopped where the bridge had collapsed. A torrent roared through the struts of the old bridge and the half-built structures of the new one that was to replace it before winter. For a few brief weeks, the weather this high in the mountains was hot enough for fireflies. Through the woods, we could see their lights dilating on and off. Higher up, the lights of Poggio stood out against the blackness of the peaks. The real history, Stefania said, was in Poggio. Our village was just a poor relation.

'I was born in Poggio,' she added, suddenly venomous. 'But I married into this place.'

A week later we visited Poggio. Padre Giuseppe, a retired priest who lived there, had agreed to say Mass in our village that Sunday, in the absence of the regular priest. He could barely remember the words, so old was he, but we couldn't help noticing how the local people treated him as one of their own. Afterwards he drove us, recklessly fast, in his battered old car, up the series of hairpin bends to Poggio.

'I'm a native of Poggio,' he said, in a broad American accent, 'but I worked as a parish priest in New York for forty years. During the war the Americans wanted to intern me as a enemy alien. I still go back there once a year to collect money for the church in Poggio. My old parishioners give me thousands of dollars every time.'

The view north and west through the mountains opened out before us. Behind Poggio a high valley, closed except in summer, led to a pass through the Apennines to L'Aquila, the regional capital of Abruzzo. Mussolini had been imprisoned up there, at Campo Imperatore, after the Badoglio coup in 1943, and before being rescued by Otto Skorzeny's paratroopers and taken north to be puppet leader of the Salo regime in the closing years of the Second World War. Mussolini himself had earlier built a lookout post above Poggio. It was still there, a gaunt ruin on a ridge high above us, used now for climbing parties to bivouac in before attempting the Gran Sasso.

Outside his own church in Poggio, a small congregation was waiting for Giuseppe. While he said Mass, we wandered uphill to the centre. There was a local government office, a pharmacy plastered with warnings about drug addiction, and a bar with stuffed local wildlife on the walls. The shops were slung with hams. Ancient stock mouldered on their shelves. Poggio was the end of the road. Beyond it, a few twisted kilometres higher, there was a ski resort only open in season. Despite the enormous mountain spaces it looked out on, it was legendary for the closed taciturnity of its residents. They even hated each other, it was said, but they would only intermarry. They had refused to have their remarkable dialect, a legacy of various occupations over the centuries, recorded for posterity by the folklore commission.

We climbed the twisted alleys of what is now almost a ghost town. Seigniorial houses, their lintels dating back to the Middle Ages, had fallen into ruin. Since the turn of the century, the place had been abandoned in waves of emigration. Crows and pigeons perched in the blackened holes that once had been windows. Planks were nailed over the doors of houses whose owners would never return. Cats had the place to themselves – there were cats everywhere. There must have been dozens around the tower where Padre Giuseppe, the old priest, lived. He left food out for them.

We watched as a woman in an alley slaughtered an iridescent cockerel. There was a taint of medieval violence about the place. The Orsinis, the papal overseers, had hung thieves here. Wolves – and there were still wolves – had savaged the sheep. Pirates, disloyal to church or state, had found a bolthole here. Something of that freedom of spirit, that savagery and aristocracy, still hung in the air. It was a place that had kept itself clear of the big powers of commerce and politics monopolizing the rest of Europe, and remained true to an original intensity of its own, leading back to a deeper past, breathing a freer air in the mountains. We were to come back to it again and again as a spiritual home for the year, just as the demoralized village a mile or two below it was our physical home.

3 ABOUT ONE THING we were certain. Whether we stayed up there a long or short time, we would be reading a lot. Half our baggage consisted of books, as many as possible about Italy. Strange though it may seem, books on contemporary Italy are hard to come by, apart from guidebooks and art history manuals. Of the many things I read about Italy before coming, only some asides of the Russian poet Alexander Blok, visiting in 1909, caught the essence of what we had seen on arrival – a crazily active modernity swarming about in the shadows of its own heroic past, as if the two had never been connected.

Our books – the bookshelf in our bedroom collapsed noisily one night under their weight – included a biography of Mussolini, *Lutheran Letters* by Pasolini, and surveys of Italian life by British authors looking through a haze of condescension brought on by food and wine. Not a lot to go on, unless our sense of Italy confined itself to regional cookery and the history of medieval art. But we were living in a mountain village, and visiting a provincial town half-proud, half-ashamed of its fascist architecture; in a region where many still bore the name Benito, where the church walls and rubbish skips were scrawled with neo-fascist slogans. We discovered that the Abruzzo had its own poet, and his works were available in English. To the shelf on the bedroom wall we added Ignazio Silone.

His early years, in a village south of where we were, had

14

coincided with fascism. As a young communist in the Twenties, he had seen the boys of his own village strutting about in black shirts. His family had had murder and torture visited upon it. In the Thirties, he had been forced into exile in Switzerland. There he had lived out the dark spasm of the war years, writing the novels of Abruzzo mountain life which, when published openly in Italy after the war, made his name synonymous with the ideals of the new left, the renewal of Italian political life that was to be disillusioned in the decades which followed. Silone himself had died in exile, but his body had been brought back and buried in his native village. That summer was the tenth anniversary of his death.

By an upstairs window, we read *Fontamara* and *Bread and Wine*. Outside, we could see the realities of village life, unchanged since Silone had represented them fifty years ago. The rival bars had guttering neon signs outside them. Lawsuits drained the pockets of the villagers. We could hear them shouting, within earshot of our window, about who owned what. And we heard the water, siphoned from the parish house, hissing away into adjacent pastures.

'America will come to Italy,' Silone has one of his fascist bosses say. Middle-aged emigrants, home for the summer, drifted in twos and threes to the bar. Dressed in loud American plaids and checks, they greeted each other with 'Howya doin'?' One or two of their daughters had already married back into the village. Others, hardly out of high school, flirted with the taciturn village boys. When the village had gone dead at two in the morning, we heard them giggling in the back alleys. If the evidence of others who had married back here was anything to go by – eternally pregnant women who had forgotten they were ever anywhere else — they would have a long, quiet life ahead of them, if anything went wrong.

There were people in the village who had read Silone. Not many, but they existed. Then there were all the others who nodded sagely when you mentioned his name, and said *Vino e Pane* as if they had read it, when in fact they hadn't. In this as in so many other respects, the village was Italy in miniature.

One day in August, we borrowed a car and drove south to his birthplace — a cloudless blue day, the traffic swarming past us on the *superstrada*, the Adriatic sea to one side and the distant blue shapes of the Abruzzo mountains to the other.

We were in a mythical midwest of the mind, dotted with service stations, tollgates and filters to ancient towns. Italy had taken on board the American propensity for unlimited, incessant movement, speed as innocence. The car, the symbol of economic emancipation, was its signal to the world that the days of emigration were over. America, as Silone said, had come to Italy. It was writ large on the landscape, in the form of flyovers, spaghetti junctions and overpasses trembling on hundred-foot-high stanchions as brittle as the construction boom that produced them. Jerry-built apartment complexes and beach hotels crowded the Adriatic coast. Fast money and property development had run riot, a new south put up overnight before government legislation caught up with it. Roofless buildings waited for the next planning amnesty, the next concession of defeat. We could see the contempt in the south for the central government in Rome, that despised arm of Piedmontese industry.

At Pescara we left the sea behind, veering wildly inland at a hundred miles an hour, with lorries barrelling past us in the outer lanes. There was a human landscape somewhere below us, had we an instant to notice it – the ancient landscape of Italy, worked by hand. Acres of corn coming to a head, fruit trees, vineyards ripening into autumn. In the heat of early afternoon we crossed the barren mountains and came down into the plain of Fucino.

Here, we were in Silone country. Across this valley floor his village women had long ago marched in the heat to the district town to protest at the diverting of their water supply, to be laughed at by the government clerks, and provoked by the fascist gangs. The sour local wine, the half an onion the boy in *Fontamara* takes as food on the train to Rome to look for a job, grew on these barren slopes. The modern road signs – Sulmona to the south, Avezzano to the west, to the north L'Aquila – defined the geography of the novels.

The plain itself was a wide, haunted space, alternately roasted under the magnifying glass of the mountain sun and shadowed by big, fleecy clouds drifting across it. Acres of crops waited to be harvested. Agriculture was by remote control, a corporate world of chemicals and combine harvesters. It was serried, organized, beautiful to come upon as we emerged from the mountains, but exclusive of the poor villages clinging to the foothills around it.

One of these, Pescina, was Silone's village. Lost halfway up a limestone gash in the foothills, it seemed to have lain down forever under the heat. Everything was closed, in an after-dinner pall. We drove past nondescript new housing, a war memorial and the Bar Silone. We left the car at the base of the hill and climbed steep streets of ghostly, roofless houses to the ruins of a belfry – all that was left of the original village, the 'Fontamara' of Silone's novel. Under the belfry lay his grave – an iron cross, a name and the dates. Socialist party wreaths, laid on the anniversary of his death, dried at the foot of the cross. The village below was hot and silent. A man in singlet and shorts wheeled a pram out of his door and down the street, accompanied by his wife, already pregnant with their next. Abruzzese villagers, Silone's people. A generation ago, they might have left for America. Now, they lived on state assistance, like the people of our village. Neither fascism nor socialism, nor the church wavering between them, had changed the parameters of their lives.

On the outskirts of Pescina, we stopped for a meal at a family hotel. Its frontage was American midwest. The linen in its restaurant was impeccable, the menu pasta, a meat course and fizzy local red wine. A family was arguing with the management about the consistency of the pasta. Was it *al dente*? It had to be *al dente*. Satisfied that it was *al dente* they, and we, ate a meal away from the heat of the day. In case we wondered which country we were in, a spaghetti western, punctuated with explosive shoot-outs and sentimental interludes, played on a screen above our heads.

On the way back, we took the inland route, driving north across the Fucino plain, past barren mountains on either side of us. The plain was fertile, bubbling with sources and springs, the underground seepage of water through porous Apennine rock. But on the plain, too, there were ruined stone houses. Contadino families had sold out to the big organizations and gone to make their living in towns as middlemen, *commercianti*. The country as a whole was washing its hands of its peasant past, in a giant collective aspiration to middle-classness. Immigrant labour, in the provinces now as well as the big cities, would do the menial work. To drive through this central zone of the Abruzzo was to see these changes – the abandoned stone dwellings in the country, and around the city of L'Aquila an encrustation of apartment blocks inhabited by those who, a generation ago, had worked the land.

We crossed to the Adriatic side of the mountains through a tunnel bored right under Gran Sasso. Entering on the barren inland side, we emerged into green Adriatic fertility twenty minutes later. In between was the dark hallucination of the tunnel itself – miles of narrow walls strung with lights, ventilation shafts and emergency telephones. The tail-lights of half Italy were in movement ahead of us, a far cry from Silone's peasants, who needed permission from their bosses to buy a railway ticket. I thought of Berardo Spina, the hero of *Fontamara*. For a brief moment, at the end of that novel, he embodies the new idea that is to unite the Abruzzo villages against the world which oppresses them: solidarity, the overcoming of petty divisions that make organized resistance possible. Driving back into the village at nightfall, with its slogans on the walls, its men not speaking to each other, its fleabitten animals scratching themselves, it was hard to feel that Berardo Spina, or the socialism Silone had conjured out of the Abruzzo, had ever been a reality, or ever would be.

4 THE WEATHER IN THE mountains grew
steadily hotter into the middle of August. Thun-
der rumbled on the ridges behind the village,
but no rain fell. We were too high up for mosquitoes, but
from first light swarms of flies buzzed, settling lightly on
our faces, making sleep impossible. Blasts of wind out of
nowhere rattled the shutters and died away. It was, they said
in the village, the build-up to the breaking of the weather
on the Feast of the Assumption, Italy's biggest holiday.

The crowds in the village had increased over the six weeks
we had been there. No foreigners, only Italians back from
Toronto. In Canada, an alternative Abruzzo existed. Such
was the binding power of the mountain communities that
the displaced villagers only married among each other. Every
second or third year they came home and the intervening
years were spent saving for the next visit. Those who had
returned this year were already counting the days left to
them.

Then there were the old women who had come home for
good. Their husbands had died, they were in perpetual
mourning. Through the hot weeks of summer, they sat in
silence at the well in the middle of the square. They were
toothless, white-haired, shapeless as sacks under black everyday dresses. They seemed to have outlived themselves, to be
looking back from beyond the grave. They had fulfilled their
role in a patriarchal society. It would be a while before we

realized that the self-effacement of these mother-figures exacted a high price from the males they had fostered and spoilt. We were living in a feminized society.

As the heat and crowds increased, so did the noise level. Situated as we were across the road from the bar, we got the worst of it. At least the others who got tired could stagger away to the quiet of their own houses at the other end of the village. Our night's sleep was reduced to a couple of hours between closing and opening times. We came to appreciate at first hand the absence of an upper limit to pure noise.

To add to the confusion, our Teramo priest moved into one room in the house for August, to give the church a presence in village affairs in those weeks, to instruct the children in catechism for their Communion later in the year, and to take his youth group climbing in the mountains. Summer was when the younger priests did their stint in the mountains. They were quickly brought face to face with their own declining influence. Our priest made it his business to be involved locally, but there was a reserve towards him always.

'They're hostile,' he said, 'because they've lost their ecclesiastical culture. It's different in the sheep villages further north.'

Although he needed only a couple of hours' sleep a night, he too suffered from the noise, especially on our account, as our reason for coming here in the first place had been a search for silence. For a while, we toyed with the idea of leaving the mountains altogether, but he advised us to wait and see if it continued into September, and in the meantime offered us a room on the Adriatic coast for a week. He was right. Soon, we were to have more than enough silence to compensate for the present bedlam.

Everything climaxed in the middle of August. All the villages around us held festivals. Looking out at night, we followed the car lights of drivers going from festival to festival, village to village, like stars gone astray in the black mass of the Apennines.

'Our festival is held in the name of the parish,' the priest said ruefully, 'yet look what it has become.'

It was the wildness in the village that troubled him. A stage was being built opposite the church. Music pounded out, day and night, from a hastily assembled sound system. Pews from the church were carried into the square to serve as seating for the audience. What he had in mind was a little innocent merriment, patronized by the church. But as the villagers well knew, he didn't live there. He dropped in once a week to say Mass, and sped away again. He didn't know what the place was all about.

'We'll have to pickle the priest,' a village woman said, 'the way I pickle the tomatoes in my jars – to keep him in one place long enough to see what is going on here.'

Lorries with stage equipment rolled into the village. North African traders set up stalls by the wall of the church. Motorcycle gangs roared up from Teramo for the day. The local boys, with their small noisy bikes, stood in awe of these mighty machines, the symbols of Italian machismo. The gangs vanished into the bar, to drink and play the slot machines. They were looking for trouble, although they found none in the village. We were to see them elsewhere in Italy, mostly when travelling in trains. Their stylistic energy, lostness and violence were to impress us again and again.

They were the ones Pasolini had written of in his *Lutheran Letters* – the so-called working class, stripped of its inherited culture, chasing a consumeristic dream beyond its means, and ripe for fascism. The tough little village boys, still innocents beside them, looked up to them as gods.

On the Feast of the Assumption, a larger than usual congregation attended Mass. Those home for the summer were making a gesture to their communal and religious past. For many, it was the only time in the year they would enter a church. In the bar we had seen a yellowed photograph from the Thirties. It showed mobs of poor but respectably dressed villagers waiting meekly outside the church for the procession to emerge. Now, their Americanized sons and daughters, wealthier than the church itself, had come back to patronize it. Through the service they came and went, in their gold chains and open-necked shirts, or strolled up the centre aisle during the Consecration to take flash photographs. They were looking at a world that awoke no resonance in them any more, other than curiosity and perhaps a certain nostalgia.

After the Mass, when the procession had moved off, the village turned its attention to the wooden stage again, the microphones, the sound system pounding out music. An old woman whose house adjoined the stage appeared on her balcony, put her fingers in her ears in a silent eloquent gesture, and went inside again.

The concert was held that evening. The performers, a folk group, a theatre group and a showband, drifted in from neighbouring villages during the day. The theatre group consisted of an extremely fat man, an extremely thin man and a young woman. They had with them the text of a

Pirandello play. We heard them rehearsing it, in high histrionic voices, behind closed doors. The folk group, singing devotional songs, sat in with them and tuned their guitars. The technology on stage was for the showband, who arrived much later in a lorry, and kept to the bar.

As night fell, the theatre group went on. They were performing a farce with metaphysical overtones, about a corrupt judge and a man who is cheated. The extremely fat man banged his walking stick on the boards of the stage and shouted '*Signor jiudice!*' every so often, while frantic costume changes went on behind an improvised white curtain. It seemed an interminable exercise, and after a few minutes' attention, the villagers got up from their seats and resumed their normal drift and conversation, as if a silent film were happening in the background. Boys on motorbikes roared through the square, dogs fought, teenagers heavy-petted beneath the stage. Above them, the actors persisted in their idealistic effort, explained to us earlier, to raise the level of consciousness in the downtrodden villages. An hour later the villagers noticed them again, just long enough to applaud them politely off the stage.

'They won't be coming back up here,' the priest said darkly, 'if I have anything to do with it.'

He had slightly better luck with the singers who followed. At least it was music, and the sentiments of the songs – uplifting, religious – accorded with what he considered appropriate for occasions like this. They even made an attempt to get the villagers to join in the chorus of their final song. It was met, however, with dour, mountainy silence. It took the high technology and flash of the showband who came on next to dynamite them out of their apathy.

The band had been drinking. In their own good time they strolled across from the bar, plugged in and tuned up. All this took at least half an hour of the time they were being paid for. They had been on the mountain circuit for most of August already and were economizing on energy. They had replicated the showbands on television who played behind the 'personalities' – glitzy suits, Brylcreemed hair, a repertoire from the English charts of twenty years ago. As they started playing, a girl vocalist in fishnet tights leapt into the centre of the stage. It gave the impression, at last, that something was happening. The teenage boys in front of the stage faced each other down in mock bravado. The girls danced with each other in tight, smug little circles. The fattest boy in the village danced self-consciously with a girl. Awed, the other boys pretended to ridicule them. Now and then the band slowed the tempo and the older people waltzed stiffly around, with the odd foxtrot or tango thrown in.

For an hour, it broke the ice. Then, with a single encore, the band broke for cover and were gone. The crowd dispersed to the stalls selling meat on sticks, dispensing free wine. Gegeto helped the priest to put the pews back in the church. No one, not even the children, went to bed until the small hours.

The following day, the weather broke. Clouds occluded the peaks and descended into the valley. The road in front of the house ran muddy and brown with rivers of rain. For a day or two, the fair persisted, under desolate skies. Then the

traders folded their stalls and left, and the stage was dismantled. The one yellow streetlight in the village was switched
on early, in the darkening square. It was the end of summer
in the mountains.

5 TWO DAYS LATER, at dawn, we waited outside the bar for the first of the civil servants' cars to appear. We were looking for a lift down to the coastal plain. Whoever saw us there would know we needed a lift. We weren't the only ones. A couple of young women on their way to Rimini were also waiting. Rimini, they told us, is the most crowded, the most vulgar beach destination, but also the cheapest. Many of the young people around here who worked in states offices in Teramo took their holidays in Rimini. They would go in a group, and there were already others they knew there, village girls who worked behind the bar counters or in the discotheques for the summer season, before coming back to the mountains in September.

Their friend Nello was taking them, and his was the first car to arrive from the upper village. He could take us too, as far as Teramo. He was a young man of few words, with a craggy face and a wildly incongruous beach shirt. And he liked to drive fast. At first it was exhilarating. Then a kind of nausea set in as we swung wildly from bend to hairpin bend. I felt my brain and stomach swaying in opposite directions at the ends of a stem, with my eyes, devouring the curves, somewhere halfway between. The women smiled sympathetically. Italian men like to drive fast, they said. Nello, with his foot on the accelerator and his mind nine curves ahead, smiled and said nothing.

The landscape, blurred with car sickness, was transfigured

in that first morning hour of late summer. Pink and yellow striations rippled through the sunlit outcrops of mountain rock. Shepherds' shelters clung like wasps' nests to the rockface. We descended to the valley floor, narrow, twisted, with its grape-clusters ripening for the September harvest, and its drills of olive trees. Nello's lights flashed on and off, acknowledging other drivers on their way to work. Everyone know everyone else in these parts, the women explained. They all worked for the state in the mornings, drove back up to their villages at one, ate lunch, then took up their real, second occupations. It was, from their point of view, an ideal arrangement. The state existed simply to pay the bills. No real input was required, just a few hours' token appearance in the office. You could bring your knitting, your children, your sick grandmother to talk to you. The job, here in the South, wasn't a serious interference in your life. It was an opportunity to socialize in town for a morning, and be paid for it by the state. In this sense, at least, the people of the Abruzzo mountains were revenging themselves for centuries of rule from outside.

Teramo, the provincial capital, had a historic core dating back to the Romans, surrounded by square miles of anonymous suburban housing, supermarkets and car parks. Its ugliness, like the ugliness of new construction elsewhere in Italy, was alleviated by the graciousness of Italian catering. Here, people knew how to sweeten the bitterness of the morning hour before work begins. The smell of fresh coffee was everywhere. No cafeteria was too small to have its starched, cummerbunded waiter. Each bar had an individualized interior design, unlike its standardized counterpart in North Europe. The giftwrapped sweets, the fresh cakes and

rolls behind glass display cases obsessively polished by catering staff, the gilt and glitter everywhere testified to what
mattered here – the ritual of eating and drinking, the
sanctity of interior, domestic life.

There were no English papers for sale at the news-stand –
more significantly, no German ones either. This was a corner
of Italy unfrequented by foreigners, tucked away on the
Adriatic side of the Abruzzo. It was Italy, provincial as all
Italy is provincial, left alone with itself, the professional
charm left out. The main newspaper on sale was the *Messagero*
of Rome, the paper of Catholic central Italy. There was no
popular press on display, as in England, but its place had
been taken by glossy fashion magazines, adult comics with
fascistic overtones, and a welter of pornography.

Our bus ride from Teramo to the Adriatic coast took forty
minutes, on a straight road lined with baby-clothes shops
and wedding boutiques. A hot sun blazed, loud cheerful
music drowned out whatever thoughts might have entered
our heads. On either side of the road, the plains, rich with
grapes, were ready to give up their harvests. The message
was clear: mindless fecundity, human happiness. Only the
memory of the pornography on the news-stands suggested
that all this felicity under a cloudless blue sky had darker
undertones. The life of the body, the myth of the Mediterranean south, was less simple than it appeared.

This idyll was interrupted only briefly, by the appearance
of a ticket inspector. Some mildly embarrassing scenes
ensued. A large proportion of the travellers hadn't bothered
to buy tickets. Why pay money to the state if you can avoid
doing so? Much arm waving and theatrical remonstration took
place, but the inspector, wearing his armour of implacability,

waded through the particulars, filled out the forms. He was still filling them out as the bus swung into its terminus at Giulianova railway station on the Adriatic coast.

We stayed a week out there, in a room the priest found for us in an old seminary. If the seminary was anything to go by, the church in Italy was in a bad way. Its buildings had fallen into disuse for lack of clerical students. Rather than abandon it, the bishops had decided to use it as a retreat centre for priests, or a kind of hotel for Catholic youth groups from elsewhere in Italy, and to keep on a minimal catering and ground staff. In the days we were there, we met both the groups and the priests. In a sense, they represented two sides of the same problem.

The Catholic lay groups seemed to be an attempt by the church to reassert its waning influence on Italian society, on the principle that, if people were no longer coming to Mass to be sermonized, they had to be reached by other means. These groups varied from loose affiliations of families holi-daying together or mountaineering under church auspices, to prayer and meditation groups of extreme intensity and self-mortification, emotionally draining their participants, creating crises of loyalty akin to the communist cells of an earlier era. There were adult groups, youth groups, children's groups. Sometimes, they were seen as reincarnations of the fascist youth groups from the time of Mussolini, when church and state collaborated. Certainly, the villagers in the mountains so regarded them.

Given the state the priesthood was in, however, it wasn't hard to understand the existence of these groups. We saw it for ourselves, one day, when the priests of the diocese gathered for a retreat. Leaving aside those who simply hadn't responded to the bishop's invitation, the dinner guests consisted of old white heads above sixty, many into their eighties, the sons of poor peasant families for whom entry into the church was a material choice rather than a spiritual vocation. Now they were bent over their plates, being served by the one or two younger priests still active enough to attend them, having left as their legacy a mass turning away of the Italian people from the church.

Our priest had spent some time in Germany, observing the working of parishes there. He had been impressed by the wealth and efficiency of the German church, but disturbed by what he saw as its heterodoxy, the inordinate voice the laity had in the running of things, the absence of traditional authority he was used to in Italy. He repeated to us the German he had learned there, grinding out the gutturals with distaste. It was an interesting experience, he said, but nothing could equal Italy.

'They found me very talkative,' he laughed. 'Too talkative. I interrupted constantly, as we do in Italy, and they angrily shouted "Let me finish!"'

One day at the beach, he introduced us to a German friend he had made, now holidaying with his family on the Adriatic. This man, a cancer specialist, was keen to spend some time in Italian hospitals. He had three extremely well-mannered blond children who spoke English fluently. He himself had achieved a perfect mastery of Italian, in just eight weeks, and was anxious to demonstrate his proficiency. Underneath his pleasantness, he was competitive, driven. We watched as he, his children and the priest shied horseshoes at a target in the sand. The priest, in his bright floral Italian beach shorts, skipped restlessly in and out of the game, his attention wandering by the minute, shaking hands and shouting greetings to people he knew. But the doctor was deadly serious, intent on winning, even against his own children. Losing interest after a while, the priest withdrew to sit with us, much to the annoyance of his friend.

'The Germans!' he said. 'They need a safety valve, they are so pressurized. Italy is their safety valve.'

Even on this relatively unfrequented part of the coast, there were quite a number of Germans. Further north, in Rimini, and inland, in Florence and central Italy, their newspapers were on sale, and signs for restaurants and hotels were in German. In places, the villages there were more German than Italian. They were tolerated as wealthy aliens who brought money. Italy, at least northern Italy, was bringing its economic migrants of the fifties home. It could look these people in the eye, or more correctly, through a mask of professional etiquette.

I had brought a copy of Dante to the beach, much to the priest's amusement. Comics, yes, but the *Commedia*? As the sun beat down and the glassy little waves broke ceaselessly along miles of yellow sand, I began to see his point. The southern summer stole irresistibly over the cognitive faculties, reducing life to a long golden dream lived out of the solar plexus, where days, weeks and months rolled into one another. There was only one season, the season of the body, which was always happy. After that, there was only death.

'When Goethe visited Italy,' the priest said to me, 'the Italians told him, "You have a sad expression on your face – it's because you think too much!"'

So I put away Dante. For a week, we swam every day in

the warm Adriatic. The beaches were still busy, but the season was on the wane. There were phalanxes of empty deckchairs, especially during weekdays, when the locals were working. In the evenings, globed lamps came on along the seafront. Sea breezes blew the first yellow leaves down, but there was still a heavy sweetness perfuming the air from the masses of flowers along the frontages. At night, offshore, the faint lights from the fishing fleets laid patterns on the darkness, and a big yellow moon dilated over the water. Inland, in the real Italy we had left behind us, there were rainstorms in the mountains. But this, the other Italy, the idyll of escape, still clung to its late summer.

On our way back up, we travelled a different route – north, along the coast, and inland to Ascoli Piceno, the capital of the Marche region just north of the Abruzzo. It was famous, the priest had said, for the white marble of its central piazza, for its Roman remains (those not vandalized by the Nazis) and for its Longobard tower. Besides, he had a friend there, with whom we could stay over. The priest, like everyone else in Italy, had a network of friends and relatives the length and breadth of the country. It was easy to see why he, like other Italians, couldn't live anywhere else. Nowhere else would the social integument be so protective.

The road north was a linkage of nondescript coastal towns clouded with dust and petrol fumes from the huge volume of traffic, commercial and private, up and down the Adriatic side of Italy. The fishing ports were still there, but somehow annulled by the *superstrada* in their own backyards. At the border with the Marche we turned inland along the river. Here, the industrial landscape intensified. There was a new prefabricated factory every few yards. The whole river valley had been turned into an industrial estate, a yard for light engineering.

'This is where the south officially begins,' the priest had told us, 'along the border between the Marche and the Abruzzo. So all the northern industrialists have moved their factories just south of the line to capitalize on the grants given by Rome to the poorer south.'

We were passing through this ferrous landscape. A long encrustation of factories, waste lots, depots and high-wire fencing, it stretched like a rusty belt all the way across Italy, and represented another failure of intent on the part of the central government to bring the disparate north and south into some kind of material harmony. We had heard enough already about their antipathy to each other, their essential difference. This was where the battle-line had been drawn.

We met the priest's friend at his apartment in the Ascoli suburbs. We had found it with difficulty, in a maze of ugly buildings thrown up beside the rubble of half-constructed roads on the side of a hill. The lucky speculator had been given a free hand by the planning authorites, he told us, and this was the result. He spoke good English – he had completed his engineering studies in Leicester and had learned it by watching television in his off-hours, and linking the conversation to the pictures. It seemed a strange place for him to be living, until he told us he was, as it were, between marriages. Anyway, as so often in Italy, the external horror was belied by the elegance of the interior.

His situation, theologically, was a finely balanced one. He was waiting for a Catholic church annulment of his former marriage, but it was difficult to see on what grounds, as he already had a child by his first wife, and the criteria for annulment are extremely rigorous, amounting, in effect, to non-consumption. His brother, however, had found him a new fiancée of whom he was fond enough to want marriage without waiting for an annulment. As this would rupture the seamless garment of his professed Catholic orthodoxy, we gained the impression that strings were being pulled on the quiet to get a declaration, which he seemed calmly to be expecting soon, that there had never been a marriage in the first place. Reality, we were to understand, would be manipulated through connections in high places.

A little while later the fiancée came, and we all went together into the centre of town. She was a warm, pleasant woman in her early thirties, openly glad to be getting married. She had spent many years being educated in a branch of medicine at the Catholic University of Rome. She came from a wealthy background and now called herself Doctoressa, but it seemed these many years of professional preparation were to be put aside for wifehood, meaning total absorption in the affairs of her husband. Both the grandiose titles and the willingness to throw them away for domestic bliss we were to come across elsewhere. She was preparing herself, socially, for life as the wife of a successful man. She had passed the test of social orthodoxy.

We strolled through the town centre in the hot night, past the lit, crowded *gelaterias*. The historic beauties of old Ascoli were floodlit from below – the tower, the bridge, the cathedral. As we passed the cathedral, she stopped and directed our attention upwards.

'See the phallus?' she asked. 'If the church has neglected

to pay the town council, it's obligatory to have a phallus.' High up, among the angels and madonnas, the gargoyles and cherubs, there was an erect stone phallus.

'Beautiful' she laughed.

We never saw this happy couple again. But the priest kept us up to date as the year proceeded. The annulment came through without a hitch. In October they married. Shortly afterwards they bought a large country house outside Ascoli, which she threw herself into decorating. And, almost exactly nine months after their wedding day, she produced their first child. It seemed a perfect ending, and life was indeed beautiful if you were well-connected, looked always on the bright happy side of things as one was supposed to in Italy, and didn't, like poor Goethe, do too much thinking.

6   IN THE SPACE OF A WEEK, autumn had come
to the village. We returned to a new silence, a
new coldness and clarity in the mountains. After
the hot summer, the forests were on the turn to a brilliant
yellow. The season of fruit-gathering was coming in. The
middle of the day was still bright and hot, but the mornings
and evenings were cool. At night, for the first time, we
needed blankets on the bed. Above us, in the attic under the
crumbling roof tiles, we heard small scurrying noises, the
sound of things dropped and picked up. A squirrel had
found its way in up there, and was storing food for the
winter.

'By the nineteenth of September,' Stefania told us, 'there
will be snow on the surrounding peaks.'

The returned emigrants had melted away. With them had
gone the spirit of summer. The silence they left behind was
both a relief and a disconcerting change of atmosphere. For
the first time, we felt in our bones the silence and isolation
of the place, a silence that would be unbroken through to
the following June. Not that everyone had left just yet.
Those from the lower valleys and from Teramo would stay
until the end of October, when the real cold came. The
children would be around until the tenth of September,
when school began. In the warm silence of autumn afternoons, the travelling clothes shops would trundle in and
park in the deserted square, with their displays of cheap

37

denim winter clothing, until the ice on the approach roads made the village inaccessible.

All of a sudden, people in the village started to notice us. Who were we? Why hadn't we left when all the others had left? Were we really thinking of wintering in that abandoned parish house, the coldest house in the village? We sat in the bar of an evening – it was still warm enough to sit out on the terrace – talking to the barmaid, Laura, who had returned from Canada to marry into the village. Local men, their eyes filmed over with alcohol, came over to take a closer look at us. They had seen us around, of course, but they hadn't made up their minds about us. They were still sizing us up.

'Those machines you have,' they said, referring to the sound of our typewriters at work in the village silence, 'we hear them chattering all day as we pass. Are you writing about us?'

'Oh no, certainly not.'

'There was an English-speaking woman once,' they said, 'who married a man from Poggio. She couldn't stand the isolation. Now she lives in Teramo with her children. Why would you come to a place like this?'

'We need peace,' we told them.

'They are great people,' the barmaid said to us, 'except when they are drunk.'

They had good reason to be curious. We were taking full advantage of the new silence about the place, and pounding away, morning and afternoon, in our upstairs rooms. Compared to the general apathy that had settled since the end of the summer season, the men chewing straws and staring out into mountain space, we must have seemed a fount of industry. The routine we had painfully and sweatily established in the summer months – I had bought wax earplugs to keep the external racket out of my head – now stood us in good stead. We were doing what we had come up here to do.

Not that the rest of the village was entirely idle, but for the men not lucky enough to hold down state jobs in Teramo, the work, such as it was, was casual. A tunnel for water and electricity was under construction up one of the high valleys behind us. And the bridge was being repaired. The lorries, which had stopped for the August break, rolled unceasingly through the village, going up with gravel, coming down with rock, raising clouds of dust as they vanished up the forest road behind the village, so we could follow their dry plumes for miles across the mountains. In the early mornings, the local men hitched rides up to the worksite on these lorries, but they were back at the bar by eleven, drinking coffee. Or there were strikes, and everything stopped for a week. Work, in short, was an occasional intrusion into a local life underpinned by pensions and government allowances. Out there was Italy, the state, an abstract idea to be exploited. The village, the visceral sense of oneness with one's friends, was what really mattered.

The faces of the friends became familiar to us – we could put names on most of them. Silvio, gaunt, consumptive and vaguely threatening; Nello, barrelchested, the tenor voice in these mountain wastes, who had taken us down to Teramo in the summer; Alberto, despised husband of Stefania, always on his way to the bar, forever fending off dogs at his heels; the white-haired man who siphoned water from our house, except when the priest was up for Mass; the impossibly

39

aged Emilio, bent double, almost voiceless, gently wheeling young children through the village on sunny mornings; Olympia, whose sister ran away with the parish priest years ago. And others, old and young, never well known to us in our time there, who became, nonetheless, a kind of Greek chorus of village life against which our private struggles with ourselves took place.

As the midsummer denseness went out of the forests and the leaves began to fall, the contours around us stood out. We were built on a series of stepped terraces, once cultivated by emigrants of long ago, now grassed over and used to pasture horses. Below the village were kitchen gardens, some cultivated to the inch, others overgrown and neglected. An asphalt road, rutted and potholed with the heavy traffic of lorries, connected upper and lower parts of the village – separate family groups, separate loyalties. Between the two parts were a few acres of pasture, some hencoops and ruined houses. The village was poised between ruin and renovation. It was too early in the autumn to bring the animals down from the mountains, and the acres of pasture were empty.

Through summer, the bar across the road had profited sufficiently for the women who had organized it as a *co-operativa* to extend their experiment to a mini-market. In September, it opened. Four young women from the village worked it in shifts, between bar and shop. At the changing of shifts, we heard their powerful voices calling each other to work, from opposite ends of the village. Every second day, carabinieri from the police station pulled up outside it. Self-important, jackbooted, bristling with small arms, they went in to satisfy themselves that the regulations governing such premises were being adhered to. Behind bar and counter, the women wore ludicrous outfits and caps, in conformity with the rules. When the police left, the women complained bitterly about the pay-offs they were expected to make, about the plainclothes 'customers' sent in to check if receipts were being given, to catch them out. Their attempt to organize, to lift the lid on village apathy, carried with it a heavy price tag.

They were to be given a trading licence – something bitterly resented by the family who ran a second bar in the village and who had strung up a neon sign of their own. This family, comprising Silvio as well as the white-haired man who siphoned water, and various tough wives and bull-headed daughters-in-law, was presided over by a sugary woman with reptilian eyes who slithered on to her balcony at the hint of any nastiness outside. Dour and powerful, feared and respected, they were the dominant clan of the village. They were campaigning for control over a public telephone. Later in the year, I felt the weight of their louring silences in the little bar they had set up for themselves, when I went there for a drink. One of the family, a nervous adolescent called Graziano, served behind the counter. As soon as he was old enough, he told me, he would be getting out of here.

Whatever complications the shop may have introduced to the village, it made our lives simpler. Without it, winter up there would have been out of the question for us. It had the obsessive cleanliness of all Italian domestic interiors, the chrome and glass surfaces of freezers and display cases wiped continually. There were never more than a few people at a time in it. It sold staples, alimentary and pharmaceutical, including, I noticed, boxes of syringes – but no luxuries. It had been set up for those, like ourselves and the village ancients, who couldn't or didn't do their real shopping in Teramo, and the prices were higher.

We lived on a tight budget, portioned out on a monthly basis. We supplemented the basics from across the road with seasonal greens and vegetables from the village itself, and settled into a dietary regime that, while not spartan, was simple. Coffee in the morning, bread and salad at lunch, and in the evening a pasta made almost invariably from a tin of tuna, some tomato purée and rods of spaghettini softened in salted boiling water, the whole washed down with cheap Abruzzese wine sold by the flagon. A simple enough diet, but luxurious compared to Gegeto, our sacristan neighbour, who subsisted on bread and pasta garnished with oil. But that was deceptive, because his refinement of palate with respect to pasta was equivalent to that of a wine connoisseur elsewhere – as we discovered when we served our version of it to him on one of his regular visits.

'*Pasta Irlandese*,' he smiled with icy condescension, a moment after tasting it.

In spite of its stone floor and its walls blackened by smoke, ours was a well-equipped kitchen. It had a cooker, an electric water heater and a washing machine. The only problem was that any two of these appliances used in conjunction with the lights would overload the system and plunge the house, suddenly, into darkness, cold and silence, until we groped to the trip-switch outside. The stove was worked off a gas cylinder. It was never possible, except by a close study of the flame, to estimate when the gas in the cylinder was about to run out. Through summer and autumn, we depended on the villagers with cars to bring us replacements from the sources of these cylinders, as far away as Teramo. As the weather got colder and cylinders for heaters became necessary, the business of deciding which cylinder, of what source and what degree of fullness or emptiness, would be best used or replaced where in the house, entered the realm of probability theory. The problem was solved when the first lorryload of yellow cylinders pulled up outside our shop, in the falling snow. From then on, all we had to do was to heave the '*morti*', the dead cylinders across the road.

In the quiet of early autumn, we had a closer look at the church. It could be reached through the sacristy door at the back of our house. The sacristy was hung with coloured vestments and altar cloths, ironed by Stefania. Gegeto, master of natural forces, provided flowers and dealt with the electricity. On the sacristy wall, a console controlled the multiple lights of the church, also the microphone and a recorded choir that roared forth at key moments in the service, giving the impression, if you were passing by outside, of a packed congregation in full voice. In fact the average attendance at Mass was five to ten old people, who, after a lifetime of being talked down to by their priests, could hardly be expected to engage in full-throated response at this stage in their lives. An earlier priest, the one who had run off with Olympia's sister, had installed this strange machine, if only to keep himself company.

It was this priest who had turned the village against the church. He had stripped it of its baroque furnishings, and modernized it into a concrete hangar, with a few bits of remnant statuary tucked away in the corner. The rest he had auctioned off, especially an ancient chalice, the most prized possession of the village. The canvasses and statues left were all worm-eaten wood and cheap gilt paint – sentimental Madonnas with a rosy nipple peeping coquettishly out, Saint Lorenzo walking his dog, cherubim who appeared to be urinating rather than hovering over celestial scenes, and irritated-looking devils with horns and serrated tails, being crushed underfoot. The lush, baroque iconography of an unlettered people – tactlessly the priest had sold it off as rubbish. Added to his other misdemeanours, and a long history of exploitation, it constituted, in the mind of the village, an indictment of the church.

Living on church property, albeit an abandoned house, begged the question of how we too would be regarded. In a way, the priest had been both our entrée to the village and a guarantee of our exclusion from certain aspects of it. Not that that mattered, as we hadn't come up there for a social life. Without knowing it, we had already, by simply staying on, done one thing right. We had made an act of faith in the village in its harsher seasons, we were prepared to share its hardships and scarcities instead of simply flitting in for the summer weeks and disappearing, as the swallows were about to do.

There was only one incident, in early September. We were reading in a room upstairs one hot evening. Most of the adults had gone to Teramo to attend a wedding. Suddenly, a gang of teenagers emerged from nowhere and began stoning the house from across the road by the bar. We switched off the lights and watched from a window. They were shouting obscenities in English, their faces distorted, hysterical, overcome by a kind of mob instinct. They must have imagined we were more frightened than we were, because when I opened the door and went towards the bar they scattered. The girl behind the bar pretended to know nothing about it, but promised to warn them off. Nothing more happened. The adults returned an hour or two later in old, dirty cars, their shirt buttons loosened from the revels in Teramo. No one apologized or alluded afterwards to the incident. It had come out of nowhere and disappeared into nowhere.

Two days later, school began. At six thirty, a bus pulled up in the sleeping piazza and tooted its horn once. We heard, in the distance, a river of light voices arguing, shouting, as the schoolgoers climbed aboard and the bus roared off to the next village on its mountain round. By eight, it would deliver its catchment of students to the *Scuola Media*, down in Teramo. For six mornings a week, the teenagers were taken at this early hour. At three in the afternoon – we timed our day by it – the bus brought them back. They vanished into their houses to eat, to study, and after brief recreation in the evenings, they bedded down early to be up at dawn the next day. It was a hard schedule, and left them little energy for distractions like ourselves.

With the departure of the children for school, the autumn really arrived. The barmaid sunned herself on the terrace after her early morning clientele had gone to work. The whole village sunned itself in a kind of benevolent timelessness, like something that had given up on the struggle for existence, or not begun it yet. Emilio trailed the babies out for a walk, or they trailed him. The travelling shops made their irregular appearances. Otherwise, all was sun and silence in those mornings. The forests across the ravine turned yellower and yellower. Gunfire boomed, as the hunting season began. The settled blue weather stayed with us all autumn, except for the high, surrounding peaks swimming in and out in their own storms, already dusted with snow. Into this blue, pristine silence we woke each day, glad if we heard a voice calling us from below the window, for we knew it was Alessandra.

7 ALESSANDRA, THE POSTMISTRESS, was our link with the outside world. Her shout meant that there was something at the post office for us – probably a parcel, since she would have brought a letter and shoved it under the door, or made it an excuse for knocking us up at the – to us – unearthly hour of eight thirty and having a cup of tea and a chat. As it was usually only a shout, though, we could breakfast in the anticipation of crossing the square a little later and signing out something interesting, like a package of new books to add to our reading matter.

She was, in fact, the only representative of the Italian state in the village – a dubious qualification. Her post office was a dark, dingy room off the piazza, with a tattered Italian flag propped against one wall, a stove and gas heater in the middle, and a much-used toilet at the back. As state jobs went, it was as undemanding as you could ask for. She arrived from her home village of Prato, five kilometres away, at eight thirty, sorted and distributed the minimal mail for the village – mostly government pensions, a few letters and postcards which she read assiduously – and knocked off at one, closing up the room and driving back to cook a meal for her own children when they returned from school.

Our arrival in the middle of the morning usually found her in the limbo between the end of her brief morning duties and her time of departure, a limbo filled by gossiping about their husbands with the local housewives or by shutting herself away in the toilet with a magazine while a small local assembly waited — we had learned the art of waiting by then. As often as not, the door was simply locked — she had gone to bargain for fruit at the travelling shop, or to visit a friend, and we went in search of her.

When we found her, she wasn't always in the best of moods. She was lunar, a moonwoman subject to the ebb and flow of emotional tides. She was small and dark, with a perfectly oval face, heavily powdered and lipsticked. She gave off signals to the world at large by the colour of her clothing on a given working day — yellow meant her manic phase, a day for playfully tweaking the crotches of the men who came to the counter, or dancing waltzes with Stefania in the deserted autumn piazza, to the music of the travelling shop. Black and red combinations, on the other hand, meant the likelihood of an existential crisis — faith, God, the fidelity of her husband — spilt out tearfully to whoever was at hand, or black moody silences, the post flung wordlessly at the recipient. The weather had a hand in all this too, and her moods were not helped by the grey morning mists into which she arrived in November.

'*Que ambiente statico!*' she spat, looking into the empty piazza, with its few ancients toiling about.

She had been postmistress in the village for eight years, unsupervised apart from the occasional reprimand from Poggio — an adequate time in which to cultivate her own eccentricities, allied to the already monumental ones of the Italian postal system. Our attempts to post the simplest of parcels involved us in antediluvian webs of regulations, from the type of string to be used, to the legal necessity for glue, to the impermissibility of including a letter and the obligation to write the address within an allocated area of x square centimetres on the parcel – often impossible, given the huge exotic Italian stamps that had to be affixed as well. Our correspondence with Ireland, Britain, Sweden and the United States complicated her life and sent her back to the statute books. Sweden? Where was Sweden again? and Ireland – or was it Iceland? or Holland? – wasn't it off the coast of Norway? Not for nothing is the Italian postal system known as the world's worst, with Tibet in second place. There were cases in the village of people receiving letters twenty years after they had been posted.

She took a jaundiced view of the village. Prato, where she lived, was a morally superior environment. Life here, she said, was degenerate. Did we know one of the woodsmen with the bad teeth was dying of syphilis? And yet he had had a second child. He was a dealer, and the village had several addicts – hence the syringes. And some of the teenagers had had two abortions already. And the young men and women lived together up here without bothering to get married, like that barmaid back from Canada living with her *fidanzato*. And they were treacherous, the villagers. They reported her behind her back, with anonymous letters to the authorities in Poggio when she shut the place up earlier than usual, and drove back home. It was a nasty place, she said, outside the laws of God or man.

She had leanings towards mystical theology. She was an ardent reader of the books of piety written by the famous Carlo Carlone of Spelo, in Umbria, and had once been to consult him in a spiritual crisis. What is life without faith? she was fond of asking. She had also, for years, consulted psychiatrists on the problem of her depressions and elations. It had cost her a fortune and the end result, she said contemptuously, was that they had told her she must 'live with them'. Resultantly, she had become acquainted with a range of uppers and downers which she took regularly – they were dispensed without difficulty to all who wanted them – and had become an authority on them. She lived, as far as we could see, completely through the heart. Motherhood – she had two children and wanted more – was essential to her sense of dignity and worth. Reproductive capacity, she sometimes said, was the measure of a woman.

'*Dove bambini?*' she was fond of asking my wife, while poking her in the stomach, feeling for the swelling. In this she was of a piece with the other village women.

Her eldest daughter, a girl of fourteen, brought her English homework to us a few afternoons in September. We were, as English speakers, a novelty up there. As the novelty changed to something approaching work, however, her enthusiasm waned. Her cartoon schoolbag, like those of all the other teenagers, told its own story. School was fun, it was a rehearsal for the all-Italian activity of just being together, of socializing. Lessons, work, were a poor second. Results were unimportant, since one's options, as an Abruzzese villager, were clear anyway: as a girl marriage and motherhood, as a boy, a job secured, if at all, by a '*raccomandazione*' from someone on the inside. I had never seen children so happily going to school as in Italy, so careless of the outcome of their studies. It left them intellectually disadvantaged, but socially, emotionally complete.

Through these lessons, we became friends with Alessandra. On dry afternoons in September and October, we walked the five kilometres from the village to eat dinner at her house in Prato. Cars braked as they passed us, and the drivers offered us lifts. The sight of people actually walking from village to village had become a rarity. There was the danger, the drivers told us, of wild dogs. They seemed to have forgotten, since the advent of the asphalt road, their own capacity as walkers on pilgrimages across the mountains – often twenty miles, often barefoot, in late summer, to remote venerated shrines of the Blessed Virgin. The completion of the new road had changed their relationship with their own land-scape.

Bright, clear, autumnal, without the oppressive heat of earlier months, it was ideal weather for walking. The air was spiced with the smell of dead leaves. Old women, balancing bags of windfalls on their heads, toiled along the road to the village. The yellow butter-and-eggs of snapdragons, the blue of cornflowers, hung on into the late autumn. Here and there on the road were the whiplashes of dead snakes run over by the cars. We smelt the warm effluvium of goats and heard their bells, as the herds moved, invisibly, through the woods above us. It was hard to tell how near or far they were, so clearly did the sounds carry. Lines of sheep flowed along the slopes below us that fell, almost vertically, into the ravine. We could hear, from down there, the torrent battering its way over the stones. In a month, the trees at the foot of the ravine would be bare, and we would see the pools and rapids of the torrent itself, freighted with icewater.

We walked in a great loop, from headland to headland. On one sat our village, behind the other sat Prato. The road between them, a *cause célèbre* of local politics, had not been im-proved by the sixteen years that had gone into constructing it. The surface had split in a million hairline cracks. There were potholes full of water, diagonal rifts and crude welts of new asphalt covering them. Pieces had broken off and fallen away into the valley. Above us, the outcrops were meshed in steel wire to prevent falling scree. The road on its tortured stanchions over the ravine bespoke fragility in the face of earth tremors. The rocks, when we touched them, flaked away in layers, like dead skin.

We lay on the second headland, looking back at our own village. A few hundred feet above it, swathed in the blue smoke of its chimneys on still afternoons, stood Poggio. Higher still were the valleys that led to passes across the Apennines, and the three peaks, from the Corno Piccolo, to the Corno Grande, and the Gran Sasso itself, lost in its own snows and weathers at ten thousand feet. We rested there, in the wild grasses, above us the high mists and occlusions of the peaks, below us the Adriatic fogs on the valley floors. We were suspended in mid-air, wrapped in a wild peace.

Prato was a wealthier village than ours. Its church, still with its baroque clutter, hadn't been vandalized, but the priests were in no better odour here than where we were. The last one had recently been removed, after years of surreptitious buggery, as a menace to the boys of the area. Apart from the church, it had a row of seigniorial houses on an avenue of pollarded trees, a war memorial that linked it to the state in a way our village never was, a clinic with a doctor in attendance twice a week, and a few shops. Wealthy outsiders from Rome, who came for the winter skiing or to escape the summer heat, had built alpine houses in the woods above it, but in the autumn it was out of season, and the only flicker of life seemed to be, as in our own village, the ominous gangs of teenagers outside the little bar, and a few groups of men playing cards inside. Had it not been for Alessandra's household, it would hardly have qualified as a destination worth five kilometres of walking to get to.

She herself took a poor view of the bar. The barmaid there was '*molto provocativa*'. Her husband, she felt, went there too often to play cards and meet his friends. Still it was there she met us the first afternoon, and took us to her house.

Her family owned a tall yellow house on the street of pollarded trees at the back of the village. Their apartment occupied the second floor. The ground floor was a storage area for ski equipment and maturing wines, and the top floor, normally empty, was leased to relatives. One entered the living room directly from outside, and the family was almost always all there – literally living, as in quarrelling, eating, keeping warm, coming and going incessantly from the houses of neighbours. A corridor led to bedrooms and a kitchen, where people went offstage for brief periods, before reappearing for fresh histrionics. Led by Alessandra herself, they were a dramatic bunch. I do not ever remember going in there when the television was not on. It dominated one corner of the room – a giant bluish colour screen – as the chimney breast dominated the other corner. Between them, on the sofa, Alessandra's husband Stefano sprawled, with a remote control for changing channels in one hand, and a *Gazzetto dello Sport* in the other. He was a tolerant, welcoming man, used to his living room being an open house. He was a tax collector for the area – a difficult job, as he admitted – and ran a mink farm on the side. He was the rock upon which this volatile family was built. The storms, largely of female domestic argument, raged around him, but

he sat them out with an air of benign withdrawal, occasionally barking at his children to be back by a certain hour.
The great emollient in all this was the television, in front of
which conversations, of whatever level of importance, broke
off as a legshow pranced on stage, an action replay was
shown of a goal between Milan and Bologna, or a young
woman, in a game of televised strip poker, removed her
brassière.

The other corner, with the chimney breast, was dominated
by the dark, silent presence of Alessandra's mother, dressed
perpetually in black since the death of her husband. She had
white hair and a long unsmiling face. When she touched
you, her hands were icy. She emanated coldness, a dissolution
of the flesh begun already, before death. With slow, automatic gestures, she fed pieces of wood to the fire, and her
one desire was warmth. It was as if, since that death, she had
ceased to live, had withdrawn beyond personality altogether.
She ate little, and answered Alessandra's irritated questions
with cold monosyllables. She was part of the family, as death
is part of life.

In the middle of all this the two children tried, in their
distracted way, to study. As an environment for intellectual
concentration, it left a lot to be desired. There were no
books, or indeed any printed matter at all except the daily
paper and a couple of screen magazines. They flitted to and
from their textbooks between eating, stoking the fire and
quarrelling over scarves or schoolbags while Alessandra
cooked, the television blared, neighbours dropped in for a
chat, or their friends flopped on the sofa and waited for
them. They were both doing badly at school, but no one
seemed too worried. Their real education, the rich socializing

influences that would get them through life more effectively than any qualification, was happening right here. They insisted, each of them, on their own diet. For the girl, that meant eggs, for the boy a type of sausage, while the rest of us ate the rabbit cooked in wine that was an Abruzzese speciality. This insistence was catered to, as a matter of course, by Alessandra, it being understood, as in most Italian families, that the child's desires were more central than the adult's. Eating at that table, piled high with salad, hunks of bread, local Pecorino cheese and bottles of lethal Calabrian wine, was like participating in a banquet where everyone can choose something different from the menu, but there is only one cook. On the other hand, the children were obliged to clear away the dishes and help with the washing up.

As a family, they were largely incurious about us or where we came from. Abruzzo was the world – you grew up, married and died in it. Alessandra had married Stefano in a church in the neighbouring valley. They had lived for years in the house of her parents. When they were old, they would live with one of their children. Intervening periods of solitary existence – that one of their children might, for example, set up in an apartment before marrying – were unthinkable to them. Solitude was an aberration, gregariousness the norm. As for privacy – the word for it simply did not exist in the Italian language.

We were grateful to Alessandra. Without understanding us, she took us into her family, who accepted us completely. She had only the vaguest idea what we were doing up there – two foreigners in a bitterly cold mountain village – and we didn't try to explain. But it hardly mattered. Many a night, from autumn through to spring, we sat wordlessly in the family circle, sated with food and wine, watching abysmal television. Words, explanations meant nothing. What mattered was to be together, to participate in the common human warmth. Through Alessandra, we touched on the true humanity of Italy, the generosity, without anything considered about it, that comes straight from the heart.

8 'WE ARE THE CHILDREN of Sixty-Eight.' Susanna smiled. 'I suppose you have heard of us by now. There are still a few of us left.'

We were sitting at the kitchen table after breakfast. Autumn had stripped the leaves from Gegeto's fig tree outside our kitchen window, and the sun flooded through the bare branches on to the oilcloth. Our breakfast was later than hers, but she was too polite not to accept the bad Italian coffee we brewed on our stove. She was up from Teramo for the day, and she had called in to see how we were getting on.

'Guevara!' she called through the window. 'Come back for me in half an half!'

Guevara was one of her three children named after dead revolutionaries. She herself was the daughter of Olympia, and we had often gone out walking with her at nightfall during the summer, when she had brought her children to live in the mountains during the school holidays. Olympia was one of the pillars of the church, who gave the readings on Sunday. Mother and daughter were opposites in that regard, but they shared the same psychic force. They were women of stature, with magnificent heads. Looking at them both, it was easy to see why that priest had run away, years ago, with Olympia's sister.

'You are on the way to becoming peasants.' She smiled. 'As for me, I love visiting the village, but I couldn't live here again.'

The village was where she had lived as a child. After school she had gone to university, not locally in L'Aquila, but to Siena, where she had studied science and become politically radicalized. She had returned, with high qualifications for research work, to the Abruzzo, where, however, certain ongoing Italian realities prevailed, such as the need for a '*raccomandazione*' to get a favoured research job. Without it, she had been passed over and the job given to someone with half her qualifications. Now, she was a teacher of science in a Teramo secondary school, married with three children, back within the orbit of her mother in Abruzzo, but with a different mentality.

'There was a time I would have seen villages like this as hotbeds of socialism,' she said. 'Now, I see nothing here except apathy, demoralization.'

She felt she had melted back into the status quo, with millions of her contemporaries. Both red and black factions of Italian political life had discredited themselves, she said, through the terrorist activities of the Seventies. Now, they had gone underground. She and people like her had withdrawn into reading and private life, keeping their own minds and those of their children alive to issues, trying to exert the tiny leverage of their individual selves against the conservative monolith of the systems they were obliged to work in, such as the institution where she and her husband taught.

'There, we are regarded with suspicion,' she said. 'For people like us, there is no promotion.'

Her husband Franco, who had been out fishing with the two other children, came in. He was raffishly dressed, bursting with energy and extroversion. Almost immediately, he took up the thread of the conversation and weighed in.

'The old political parties are dead,' he said. 'There is no politics now but environmental politics. The big issue is the environment – consider this village, for instance. In 1986, there was Chernobyl. The Italians say nothing in Italy was affected. Yet all through the Apennines the bees died or gave no honey in the apiaries, including the apiary of my mother-in-law here. It was necessary to buy a whole new apiary.'

'The trouble could have come from America . . .' Susanna put in.

'It doesn't matter where it came from,' he continued. 'Nature in Italy is dying. The birds have been shot from the forests. The fish are radioactive. Half of Eastern Europe is dying . . .'

'He's a green communist,' Susanna said affectionately. 'As far left as you can get – far to the left of the communists themselves, if that is possible. There are only three of them in Teramo. They have a pretty hard time.'

We had already heard of Franco. The priest had referred to him once, to his activities in Teramo, with a smile of gentle condescension, as if to an incorrigible eccentric. But the priest's attitude to most things not of the church was gentle condescension. There was, for instance, the question of Pasolini.

'Now Pasolini,' Franco insisted, 'was one of the few writers to express the crisis of Italian life. He felt that a proletarian culture, of the body as well as the spirit, which had existed for hundreds of years, had been degraded in two decades into consumerism, ruled by television and money. Look at the obsession, even in this village, with the poor imitations of designer labels! And the rubbish they watch on television.

No, Pasolini saw that Italian tragedy before anyone – saw the people's loss of cultural identity.'

I had asked the priest one day about Pasolini, one of whose collections of poems, *Per la Chiesa Cattolica*, I had found lying around with other abandoned texts in the house. A smile of gentle condescension. Pasolini, he said, was an intelligent man in many ways, but tormented, always tormented, by his homosexuality. That was the main thing about Pasolini.

'It would have been better for Italy if the popes had stayed in Avignon,' Franco said. 'We might have evolved more naturally.'

Olympia came in, with a box of assorted vegetables from her garden below the village. A gift for the house – or was it the church? Behind her came her husband Carlo, a gentle electrician who had helped us with wiring problems. She had presence, Olympia. She was the unofficial headwoman of the village during the summer. Her piety was tempered by a strain of earthy humour.

'Before we lived in this village,' she said, 'we lived in a much wilder place in the mountains.'

'I remember,' Susanna smiled. 'I was very small at the time. One morning, I opened the door of the house and outside was the carcass of a sheep a wolf had killed and tried to drag away.'

'You are the mountain girl,' Franco said, stroking her hair, 'the mountain girl.'

It was the first act of affection between a man and a woman we had seen since coming into the village months ago.

*

Not everyone thought of the village as a graveyard of socialist illusions. For instance, there was Cesare. He had a little tractor, the motor of which he left idling for hours on end as he shinned up a pole and did the wiring for the new neon sign of the *co-operativa*, outside the bar. That was his afternoon self, his morning self having put in the prescribed number of hours in the state office in Teramo. His wife Franca, between walking their two baby girls in the emptiness of the mornings, put in shifts behind the counter of the *co-operativa*.

We were absorbed into their lives by simple osmosis, being around the village and grativating towards those we could most easily communicate with. We began to visit their house, sometimes for lifts down to town with Cesare in the early morning, and sometimes to eat together.

The house they had moved into was typical of the village as a whole. In the early days of their marriage, they had shared it with Cesare's father – a difficult situation, until he had moved out. The old stone exterior had been left, while they continued to modernize it from within, room by room. The walls were thick, the windows small and the internal spaces small, with warmth in winter emphasized. They had lined the living room walls with pine and fitted branches into the walls around the table. They had reduced the hearth to a small modern fireplace. A large television screen stood opposite the table, with the telephone immediately beneath it, into which they spoke apparently without difficulty as the television blared overhead. With two small children, the living space was a clutter of soft toys and tricycles. A goldfish swam distractedly back and forth in front of the window. The racket of crying children, meals being served and cleared

61

away, visitors arriving and departing, the television, the telephone, was incessant. Privacy, with the possible exception of the bathroom, was non-existent. It was a classical Abruzzese household.

In certain respects, however, the domestic atmosphere differed from other mountain houses. The walls were ablaze with posters denouncing war and the pollution of the environment. And upstairs, alphabetically arranged according to author, they kept their books. They were the only people we knew in the village who had read Silone, the socialist poet of these mountains. They had involved themselves in the village as a kind of community project, and Cesare had recently become one of its representatives in the commune in Poggio. Aesthetically, politically, they had made their home here for conscious reasons.

It ought to have been ideal, yet the sense of alienation persisted, differently for each of them. He was too well educated in a peasant village, she was from elsewhere in Italy. They had met up north, when he was on holiday in Turin and she was working in a hotel there. After a brief, rather unreal courtship – she now spoke dryly about his 'angelic' good looks – they had married and come to live in the Abruzzo. She quickly discovered that the southern ethos, especially where women were concerned, was altogether different from that up near the French border. Before they had had a chance to get used to each other, living still in the shadow of his father, a child had arrived. Now she found herself isolated from her family and background, wheeling an infant and a toddler in the cold sunshine, suffering the closed, taciturn stares of the local women.

'I have no friends here,' she told us. 'The face of the

village is deceptive. They pretend to be friendly and sneer behind my back.'

She was still a young woman, but already her clothes and her physical appearance bore signs of neglect, of someone whose attractiveness no longer counts for anything. Cesare's political enlightenment did not extend into the area of relations with women. There, his attitudes were strictly traditional. Romance was one thing, marriage another.

'It is easy for him,' she complained. 'He goes to an office each morning and drinks coffee with his friends. I am left here with the children and no one to talk to.'

It had been Cesare's idea to live in the village in the first place. He was following through a theory in his own mind, with the reluctant aquiescence of his wife. His theory was that life in the mountains would be cheaper, that it would be healthier for his children to grow up in unspoilt natural surroundings, and that upon the village he could project the activism developed out of his studies in political science, years ago, in L'Aquila. Looked at from his own point of view, his theory was succeeding on all three counts. A kind of educated egotism blinded him to his own isolation within the village, inured to apathy, suspicious of attempts to raise its consciousness. No, life was perfect. When we called round early in the mornings for a lift down to Teramo, he was brimful of good cheer, smothering his tiny daughters in kisses as he went out of the door to begin another theoretically perfect day, balanced between work in the town and the free, healthy life of the mountains.

His wife, the x factor in the theory, he ignored completely.

*

63

Of the people of our generation in the village, however, Laura the barmaid, was nearest the norm. One Monday morning in early September, after the departure of the summer visitors from Canada, we found her behind the counter of the sunlit, empty bar, staring moodily into space. The day before, she had gone with her parents, who had departed for Canada the same evening, to be married in the registry office of the Poggio commune, to Pino, her local boyfriend with whom she had been living for the past two years.

'As far as we are concerned, it is a formality,' she said a little anxiously. 'Does marriage change anything?'

We answered evasively.

She was twenty-one. She had met Pino on holiday here when she was seventeen. After the previous day's ceremony they had gone with a group of friends to a seafood restaurant down on the coast in Pescara, said goodbye to her parents and come back up to the mountains with his ailing, aged father, with whom they were still sharing a house. And that had been it. There would be no honeymoon. This Monday morning was the morning after, the beginning of the rest of her life.

About Pino she could be sure of one thing. He wouldn't run off with anyone else, for the simple reason that he lacked the energy. He was a young man of fabulous taciturnity. He carried himself with a stooped, elderly gait, his hands clasped behind his back, his eyes on the ground. I used to watch from my window in fascination as he turned the fifty yards from bar to railings, railings to house, into an epic voyage. He had early learned the essential village art of living at a lowered metabolic rate, diffusing the burden of empty time.

He was twenty-eight, and already reverting to the condition of inanimate matter. He promised to be an ideal husband.

In Laura, he had found an ideal partner. Her favourite activities, she told us, were reading television magazines in bed, and watching television in bed. She had the tank-like maternal solidity of her mother, a woman who had reared a family of seven in the Italian quarter of Toronto. Like her mother, she was a woman of few words. She was hesitant, even inarticulate, in two languages. And like her mother, she was growing heavier, more biologically centralized, over time, and had by her side a quiet, ineffectual man.

Pino, at least, was being paid for his inertia. He too had landed a government job in Teramo. All autumn he rattled back up the mountain after work in his little car, with something for the house, lengths of wood or an appliance, strapped to the roofrack. When we visited their tiny residence built into an outcrop of rock – made into a feature architecturally – we were amazed at the refinement of its internal design and decor. Whatever else, they knew how to make a home.

Besides Laura, there were other young women at work in the new *co-operativa*. Silvia, a thirty year old who lived with her parents in the house by the bridge, came every afternoon with her knitting. Through autumn and winter she knitted the tedium of hours and days into long woollen gansies for the others. Paula, back from her summer job in Rimini. Claudia, her sister, who was *fidanzata* to a handsome, much older man who lived with his mother and was about to take early retirement from his office job in Teramo, to concentrate on sheepfarming in the mountains. They had been *fidanzata* for years already. It continued to puzzle us, this condition similar to but not the same as 'engagement', involving a looser commitment and a seemingly indefinite period of time. But it fitted in well with the capacity in the village for waiting, the young women sewing together in the long intervals between customers, exchanging gossip, and returning to eat meals at the homes of their parents. If they weren't married, they would live at home forever.

Laura soon brightened up, after her initial depression. She had a remarkably clear idea of what she wanted, even if not the power to express it verbally. It was in essence a reversion to the slow-paced, biologically determined village routine, after the high metabolic rate of the Italian quarter in Toronto. School had left little residue in her mind. Soon, the other women in the *co-operativa* had taken her off the cash register and put her on such manual tasks as distributing and collecting the gas cylinders in houses like ours. What she did know, however, was that she wanted children, that she was happy around children, and that soon she would have her own children. There was an ageless sanity in her withdrawal from the larger world. We watched her growing fatter by the month as she played with the local children in front of our house. She was deeply speechlessly happy. In the village, she had found her home.

9 SMALL AS IT WAS, OUR church had two sacristans. We heard them arguing while we worked upstairs in the warm autumn days. They had access through the ground floor to the sacristy, and it was there the arguments took place. They were one-sided, as only one of the participants was articulate. We heard Stefania's shrill voice as she tore strips off Gegeto for some stupidity connected with flowers, electricity or one of the natural forces he had failed to bring to bear on the organization of church affairs. He was the earth genius, she the possessor of piety. Listening to them from upstairs was like overhearing two sides of the Catholic psyche, locked forever in combat.

Gegeto, our neighbour, had lived for most of his life in Rome. He recalled with approval the massed crowds roaring in response to the Duce when he spoke from his window on the Piazza Vittoria. Order, authority, the destiny of Italy. After the debacle in 1945 he had gone on working as he always had, as a physical labourer, and his fascism had gone to ground. Old, white-haired, but still full of vitality and strength, he had returned to his native village, his need for authority satisfied by service to the church. Alone of the village, he had an excellent relationship with the priest, who often brought him up an old suit on Sundays. After Mass, over coffee in the kitchen, the priest bantered with him in a light, condescending manner. These brief sessions, which were the only ecclesiastical intrusion into our lives, were the

67

priest's way of holding court in the village once a week, to his few adherents. As he drove off, waving regally to a sullen populace, we watched Gegeto running alongside to catch his parting witticisms, and doubling up with laughter in the empty piazza.

Not that the villagers held this against Gegeto. He was bone of their bone. He had admittance to any of their circles. It wasn't his beliefs that admitted him, but his engagement with physical matter; the manipulation of stone and wood, knowledge of the ways of electric power and the earth's capacity to nurture green energies. Inarticulate in the language of church and state, he spoke the dumb *lingua franca* of physical necessity, which the whole village understood. A broken woodstove, a short circuit, a grave to be dug and a body buried. Unlike the empty lives of those who sometimes laughed at him, his was energized by real problems. His hands, his box of tools, would authenticate him to the end of his days.

In the evenings, he got blissfully, benignly drunk. Alcohol, which brought out a streak of violence in the village men, had a quietening effect on him, as if his inner core, unlike theirs, was calm to begin with. Owing to our mutual inarticulacy in the same language, we never exchanged more than a few words of greeting by way of conversation. When I entered the bar of an evening, he turned to the others with a pitying expression on his face.

'*Non capisce niente,*' he told them.

Our status, in each other's eyes, hovered somewhere between genius and village idiot.

*

If he had one kind of genius, Stefania had another. It took a while to discover, beneath the blue-rinsed hair and gold sandals of a fifty-year-old mincing her way through life. She had dress sense, and it set her apart from the exhausted slovens of her own age who looked askance at her, and whom she ignored.

Childless, she lived with her husband in a condition of crackling, asexual electricity that intrigued and excited the whole village. They had elaborated a system of mutual exclusion while still living together. When he was upstairs watching TV, she was downstairs watching TV. When he was in, she was out. She was a wife to him in the sense that his socks were seen hanging out to dry from the upstairs window. He was a husband to her in that his feet protruded from beneath the chassis of her little car, which he was always repairing. He held her in voluble contempt, she held him in silent contempt.

When they were first married, they had gone to America. There, they found themselves working all night in canning factories, in freezing weather, struggling with a strange language they could never master. She had cracked, and asked to come home to her mother and sister. After a couple of years he had relented. Back in the Abruzzo, they had invested their savings in a *pizzeria* at the ski resort. It was to and from there that she drove every day, through wild mountain weather, while he settled into an afterlife of failure, buttonholing whoever would listen to his side of the story. A practical, financially realistic woman, Stefania held the reins. Her strangeness took another form.

Attached to her mother, she kept only the company of

women, and had towards men a detached, polite reserve behind which lurked an icy contempt. Elegant at fifty, she must have been stunning in her youth. Her husband had stumbled, innocently, into a steel trap. Divorce being unacceptable in the village, he was living with his terrible mistake. Whenever she could, she spent time with her mother in Florence. The rest of the time, business apart, she lived in a fantasy world of girlhood before twelve (which didn't preclude savagely earthy comments on her husband's physical attributes) and a village life that never was, except in her own mind. She had, in a different way from Gegeto, found her way back into something like a collective unconscious, the folk memory of the village.

This she expressed in her naïve paintings. She was a naïve painter of some repute. It was hard to determine how much repute, but the walls of her living room were covered with citations and photos of award ceremonies. There were brochures for exhibitions, with forewords by presumably well-known critics. This was her other life, an upsurge of psychic expression through the dailiness of village life. She kept it, appropriately enough, in the darkness of the cellar beneath her house.

She took us down there one day. There were canvasses everywhere, amalgams of innocence and horrific violence, which she showed us daintily and detachedly, as if they had been painted by someone else, long since carted off to a lunatic asylum. Each had a harvest festival, a religious scene or the village itself, snowbound, castellated as in the fifteenth century, as a background. Some were weirdly lit with an asexual violence. In the foreground were trees full of hanged men, their genitalia cut off. It was as if the dark, savage life of the middle ages had come to life in her mind, with a ripple of psychic disturbance running through it.

At fifty, she still saw herself poised on the edge of dizzying adolescence, a violet waiting to be plucked. The knowledge of sterility and impending death must have been somewhere at the back of her mind, but she never showed it, preferring the illusion that life had not yet happened, was still about to happen. Once or twice that autumn, on wild October nights, we accompanied her to the country dances down in Montorio. It was a strange experience.

She danced incessantly, from the first to the last dance. The music, consisting of a single cassette, repeated itself endlessly – waltzes, tangos, and foxtrots – all of which she executed perfectly with her partner of the moment, her face expressionless, her feet in their gold shoes pounding, with a life of their own, the hard wooden boards of the cleared floor. She seemed to experience neither pleasure nor pain in these dances, to which she returned obsessively, week after week. It was more like a need to project herself into the atmosphere of a lost past, a chance in life missed long ago. Certainly the lost past clung to these country dances, which the mountain remoteness of the Abruzzo had preserved against discotheque culture. We sat to one side, watching her circle stiffly with the various suitors she kept at arm's length, while the tiny farmers' wives and their huge abstracted husbands, heads in the clouds, swung with a kind of old-fashioned zest.

These, then, were our two sacristans. On Sundays, Stefania delivered white, freshly laundered linen to the church and arranged the cut flowers Gegeto brought from his garden. At the appointed moment in the Mass, the priest nodded to her and she tripped up the aisle like a schoolgirl, watched narrowly by the half-dozen ancient women in black who made up the congregation, to read from the gospel. Her voice, a childish singsong, sped along the lines with complete disregard for their meaning, or the natural pauses for breath. The priest sat back, watching the work of his two sacristans. In their way, they were being faithful to him. But in both of them there was something older, darker, more savage and vital, where their real allegiance lay.

We were living through the end of a certain kind of religion, and we watched it on the wane. Its churches, here in the mountains, were neglected ruins, its congregations had long since vanished. Sullen and inverted through the village was, it too was experiencing the spiritual adulthood of the world. In the dusty old parish register, we saw entered the baptismal dates of those around us now grown up and loudly atheistic, corroded by the bitter realities of village life. Beyond the mix-Sixties, the entries grew fewer and fewer. Some of the children still took first communion, after a summer of instruction by the priest, but then they disappeared forever from the church, as from an irrelevance.

The older generation of priests, who had entered the church as a meal ticket, were dying out. Their personal qualities, demonstrated by what had happened in our village and in Prato, aroused only contempt in the local people, who once had regarded them with fear and deference. The new generation appeared equally unsuitable. With the drop of vocations, the church was admitting anyone and everyone. A fair proportion of the current priesthood were misfits, people with an outright incapacity for ordinary life.

Occasionally during the autumn, the priest called in with one or other of these misfits. He was taking them on his mountain rounds, a familiarization tour of the priestly life. I remember one in particular, a member of the fascist party who the priest was trying to win over for the church. He was young, small and singularly unhappy – dressed entirely in black on both occasions we met him. I was interested to note his facial resemblance to one of the irritated devils crushed underfoot by our local hero Saint Lorenzo, whose statue reposed in the church. Shortly, he disappeared forever but the priest reappeared, indefatigably, with another horror, an effete young homosexual, recently ordained but still living with his mother in Pescara, who insisted on speaking only French. It was not hard to imagine the likely reaction to him in villages like ours.

Apart from misfits, there was the priest himself. A man of extraordinary goodness, from a Florentine professional family, he had come late to the religious life. He was a churchman to his bones, and a workhorse. He was so exactly what the church wanted that they were draining every ounce of use they could get out of him. His hair, in his late thirties, was already greying. He had already been ill with stomach complaints, loss of voice, nervous prostration. Often, after a meal at our house, he slumped unconscious in his chair for ten minutes, to catch up on his lost sleep. Yet for all his integrity, and his many acts of individual kindness in the village, he was not getting through to the people. The church was God. God was the church. Obedience to its laws and institutions was obedience to God. By this logic, most of the village was damned. The few left at Mass were to pray for the many who were not, the imperilled souls. In the

73

house one day, we came across yellowed copies of an old circular issued years ago, criticizing the village for not sending a representative to the bishop's inauguration in Teramo, and attacking them for the general sinfulness of their lives. Reading it, while ourselves living in the village, was a depressing experience.

It was the time of year when the old people in the mountain villages had their confessions heard in preparation for the Day of the Dead. On that day, the relatives of the dead, wherever in Italy they happened to be living, would return to their local graveyards to commune with their deceased. One bright autumn afternoon, when the yellow oak forests were roaring in the breeze, we drove with the priest to a nearby village where he was hearing confessions. He had his windows up, and cassettes of inspirational music plugged into the dashboard. Our glass bubble of devotional ecstasy floated through the savagely twisted mountains, the ruined chapels and abandoned shrines. The village we would get to was just a bar with a jet bead entrance and a couple of one-armed bandits. The rest was rock, and blowing grasses, a life twisted out of shape by the harsh necessities of the mountains. The old still offered it up to God. The young ran away from it, to Rome and Milan.

10 IN OCTOBER, THE QUESTION of wood arose. Through that fine autumn we had heard the sound of axes chopping and the whine of electric saws in the village. We had seen our neighbours at the back of the church neatly stacking their logs, and the warm yellow of these sawn-off ends began to seem almost lovely to us. In fact, those who were at work on their woodpiles this late in the autumn were the laggards. Most of the village had bought its wood from the local dealers the previous spring, stacked it green and wet under lean-tos by their houses and let it dry through the hot summer months to be ready for use now. The priest had advised us to find ourselves a local dealer and buy in a few *quintales* for winter.

The message came home to us when the blue calm of autumn was interrupted, just once, by a low grey drizzle that settled over the village, hushed and occluded the mountains, and reduced visibility to a hundred yards. We sat shivering in front of an empty stone hearth, our feet damp from the road outside, our heaters without gas cylinders. A dead leaf blew down the chimney, a foretaste of winter. There was nothing for it but to go to bed until the weather cleared, and then start looking for wood.

We began, rather naively, with the kindling. We had seen old women at the edge of the village breaking off branches of trees with their horny hands, and tying the lengths of fine wood into bundles. Where the broken bridge was being reconstructed, there were woodchips in abundance. When we went walking in that direction, we brought refuse bags in our pockets and filled them on the return journey. But most of our kindling we collected on afternoon walks in the woods above the village.

There were old paths up there, beyond where the road petered out. It was the time of fruit-gathering, and the time when the animals were being brought down from their summer grazing. We were rarely alone in the woods, with the sounds of other people crashing about, and the thin, invisible tinkling that told of herds nearby. We came on open grassy areas scented with wild herbs, where once there had been cultivation. Now they were fenced in for sheep, and guarded by massive white dogs, who slept in the middle of the flock with one ear open, and picked us up preternaturally long before we arrived. We took our time along those twisted paths, gathering wild berries to make jam with, flinging sticks into the trees that were heavy with sweet chestnuts. Half the women of the village were out, and the paths were littered with empty yellow cases. The women had their hidden places, which they jealously guarded. Between kindling, nuts and berries, the dry October woods were a hive of activity. One day, we even saw our squirrel, a blur of chocolate and cream, skittering home through the leafless top branches of the trees. When we had as much wild fruit and kindling as we could carry, we started back down to the village as the light began to fail, through a dry golden haze of ripeness and stillness, in which the whole of our summer and autumn seemed gathered up and suspended.

There was a rank smell of goat in the fields around the

village and the roads were clogged with sheep on the move, solid masses of sheep moving with one will, the lame staggering twenty paces behind, the lambs carried upside down by the shepherds. The dogs, trained to attack strangers, were nervous of us and we of them. The sheep, thousands of them from the surrounding heights, were penned for a day or two close to the village, and driven off in lorries to the Adriatic plain. For days on end, the lorries rolled past our windows, three tiers high, so that from upstairs we sill found ourselves eyeball to eyeball with frightened sheep.

The horses, too, were being brought down. Our outside tap, through the hose under the road, had become their water supply. The water was hissing down from the attic twenty-four hours a day. Combined with the noise of the squirrel above the ceiling – Gegeto had offered to guillotine it for us, but we refused – we needed earplugs, at times, to get any sleep. The horses, insecurely corralled below the village, often broke loose at night and roamed freely, adding to the disturbance.

With sheep, goats and horses being channelled through it, the village in October became a quagmire of mud and droppings. The horses, in particular, brought out a streak of bestial cruelty in the men and boys. With the exception of one magnificent stallion, they were a neglected, mal-nourished lot. As they backed away nervously from the horseboxes, they were kicked and savagely beaten around the eyes and neck with sticks as thick as clubs. There was some idea of using them to give rides to visitors the following summer, but what would be left of them by then was hard to imagine. But they kept coming, the old, the pregnant,

77

the dangerously skittish, down from the mountain, a clatter of hooves striking sparks on the road outside our house, and the cigarette in the mouth of the man riding herd on them dilating red in the darkness.

When we got back to the village one day, with our bags of kindling, Silvio was waiting for us on a bench outside the church. By that stage, our search for wood must have been evident to the entire village. He stopped talking to his companion on the bench, approached us and motioned to a large woodpile between his house and the back of the church.

'If you need wood,' he said, 'I can give you a supply.'

At the scent of unusual conversation, the snake-eyed woman of the family slithered out on to her balcony to watch.

We were uneasy with Silvio. He was darkly reserved, the wild man of the village, fêted and esteemed. He was gaunt and emaciated, with dark intelligent eyes in which violence slept like tinder. He embodied the spirit of the village – taciturnity, erupting into violence now and again, like something too long victimized, lashing out in revenge. He was more complex than that, however. There was a gentle, henpecked side to him, ruled by his tough, realistic wife, who held the house together through his bouts and excesses. His two children, a saintly elder daughter and a nervous, crying younger one, were loners who played together – we heard their ball bouncing against the back wall of the church every evening. He was, in short, a superior personality, shedding a luciferean light, a glow of spiritual anguish over the dull idiocy of the friends who egged him on, half in admiration, half in fear and contempt. All this we had picked up simply by being about the place, exchanging the odd remark. When he worked, he was a dealer in wood, cutting it in the forests far back in the mountains, driving it to Teramo in his battered blue lorry. It was in this connection he was approaching us.

'Go to your house and wait,' he said. 'I will bring you some wood immediately.'

A few minutes later, he arrived at the back door, with a wheelbarrow full of dry, mossy logs. Several wheelbarrows later, we had a couple of *quintales* stacked in the kitchen. We were about to pay him, but he waved the offer aside.

'*Per la chiesa,*' he muttered. 'And take what you need from the big woodpile.'

Although the October weather was still balmy, we decided to light an experimental fire. It taught us a number of things straight away. The first was that the supply of kindling we had would be burnt away in a couple of weeks, unless augmented by cotton soaked in alcohol. The second was that the chimney, as we had been warned, had the worst draw in the village.

Within minutes, we could barely see each other through the blue smoke in the room. Only a blast of draught, when we opened the door from the kitchen into the unused parlour, partly dispersed it. Our big stone hearth was far too open. It would need something nailed over the top to increase the updraught. In the succeeding days, the house was visited by a small delegation consisting of Olympia, her husband Carlo, Gegeto and one or two others who had taken an interest in our prospects in the coming winter in this famously cold dwelling. Gegeto excepted, they were all moving to Teramo for the winter, having spent the summer working their kitchen gardens and doing what repairs were necessary on their mountain houses. It was not a good place for the elderly to winter, or those, like Olympia, prone to arthritis. The delegation brought with it a large piece of tapestried cloth, heavy and coarse, which they nailed in front of the fire. The result, when we got the fire going again, was not perfect, but a lot better than before.

Though they didn't say so directly, they were troubled that we had entered into dealings with Silvio. If we had approached them, they said, they would have found us a better dealer, though by now there was only green wood for sale. Stefania was already having trouble with green wood in her stove. All the dealers were robbers in some way, they said. For who but the dealer himself knew how much wood he was delivering to you? But there was Giambattista, perhaps we could still ask Giambattista. But the priest had already asked Giambattista, who had said yes, of course, and then forgotten the whole matter. So we were stuck with the ambivalent arrangement we had made for the winter. When we explained to the priest, on one of his rare visits, that we had not been allowed to pay for the wood, he shook his head and smiled condescendingly.

'He knows what he is doing,' he said.

From Alessandra, a few days later, we heard the background to this act of generosity. It seemed that the previous winter, Silvio's household had been in a state of collapse. He would have had to sell up and leave had not a sum of money been raised. The priest, on his own initiative, had raised this money and Silvio had been baled out. The offer of wood was an atonement, a salving of conscience. We, who lived in the village and knew it perhaps better than the priest did, took a less satisfied view of the outcome than he did. These were poor people. There was little room for generosity in their lives. We had established a false relation, in the web of relations that made up the village. There could be a backlash.

For the moment, however, the problem of the wood was solved. The weather continued fine through October, the whole mountainside turning yellow. There were piles of leaves on the ground, but many of the tough little oak trees kept their foliage right through the winter. In the mornings, in the places of shadow, white hoarfrost bristled on the dead vegetation of the ditches, but in the sun it was hot. The sun rose and set in a shorter arc in the mountains behind the village. At night, in the deep black of interstellar space, we followed the Plough on its way round the wheel of peaks surrounding us – now upended over a peak, now vertical beside the gable end of a village house in the dead of night. We could feel the earth, over week and months, wheeling us towards the solstice.

We had time and space. We followed the logging trail above the village far back into the mountains. It was powdered with white dust from the endless passage of lorries through summer and autumn on the tunnel construction project. The vegetation, for the first mile or so, looked blasted, dusted over. The slopes above the track had been stripped of trees by the loggers – a moonscape of dead trunks, with woodpiles by the road ready to be carried away. We heard the rasp of electric saws, and watched the tall young trees groan as they keeled over and subsided with a soft crash into the forest. Frightened by the vibrations, lizards skittered into the dry crevices.

The roar of water in the valley gave way to a weird, waterless silence, then resumed again. The torrent was emerging and disappearing in the soft, porous rock of the Apennines. Beyond the tunnel construction site, three miles deep in the mountains, it petered out altogether, and we found ourselves following a dry watercourse on rising ground through the yellow light of a vast beech forest at the end of autumn. The ground was littered with beech nuts and heavy with the undisturbed leafmould of years. It was a place of solitude, and the deep, almost frightening silence of still woods, unpeopled and birdless, floored with wild cyclamen. Landslides had gashed their way through the trees, leaving huge boulders. Higher up, the trees themselves were warped and hooped from old winters of ice and snow on their branches. If we went on, we would reach the tree line. Beyond that were the high pastures, sloping up to the barren scree of the peaks.

Lost in their own dark weather, the peaks themselves were off limits until the spring. We had often watched the rockclimbers, from all over Italy, rehearsing for them on the outcrop of rock behind Poggio. Roped intricately to each other, they stemmed up the cracks in their designer climbing gear, hammering steel spikes into the crevices, moving balletically in unison against the force of gravity. It made me queasy to look at them. Only a while back, in early autumn, a young friend of the priest had been killed up there. After concussing himself, he had continued to climb and had lost his balance higher up. The Corno Grande claimed lives like that every year.

By mid-afternoon, so late in the autumn, it got cold and shadowy up there. The beauty was desolate, inhuman, something out of Shelley's *Epipsychidion*. In blue space far above us, the pair of ravens that lived on one of the high ridges floated in slow figures of eight about each other, hunting. We saw them drop suddenly deep, deep into the valley, and begin their slow rise again, spiral by spiral on steadied wings, wafted upwards on invisible thermals, until they reached their hunting altitudes again. They were the only two birds in that vast area of mountain. Lower down, an occasional jay flashed yellow through the trees, but it was the hunting season, and the birdlife that had not been shot had gone deep into hiding. It was said that the Italian cities in autumn were aswarm with birds, guided there by a collective instinct for safety. But here, since the swallows and swifts had departed for Africa, there was little or nothing. Sparrows and songbirds, for the hunters, were delicacies on a platter.

Work on the tunnel construction project was about to stop for the winter. The endless rolling of lorries that had accompanied our stay in the village through summer and autumn, was about to cease. And the last of the summer residents had closed up their houses and moved down to Teramo. It was as if the various levels of sound that we had known through the summer and autumn had been stripped away one by one, as the village reverted to an original mountain silence and isolation. Ironically, it was just then that the road connection to Poggio was restored, and our few commuters to Teramo, spared their detour through Prato, drove across the new bridge, through the first light snow shower of winter.

11

AT THE START OF NOVEMBER, we made our first trip out of the village for two months. We had business in Umbria, three hours' drive to the north. Without a car, however, three hours through the mountains was a whole day's journey – a lift down to Teramo, a bus trip to the coast and three different trains. It was easy to see why the Abruzzese locals relied on private rather than public transport. After four months of freedom in our stone house, energized by the warm physicality of the Abruzzo mountains, we were going to Perugia, to earn ourselves the bread to do the same through the winter.

We left the village at first light, when only the cats were awake. It was still only eight when Cesare dropped us off at the centre of Teramo. The streets were alive with school-children – sometimes it seems all Italy runs on the energies of children. There were smells of roast coffee, and the newsvendors's stalls were thick with morning editions from all over Italy. We had entered history again.

The coastal plains had changed since the late summer. They were brown, ploughed over, and spread away in flat wintry acres broken by marches of bare trees. The short southern winter had come to the coast, and these dark acres spread all the way down through Apulia. They would stay dark through December, and start turning green again in January.

An east wind blew off the Adriatic. It threaded mists and

coastal fogs up through the valleys to where we were in the mountains, but down here the clouds scudded inshore and the rain clattered in blinding sheets against the windows of the train as it rattled north to Ancona, through resort towns closed for the winter. A big sea cannoned off the surfbreak, and whitecaps spread away to the horizon. In the grey middle distance, lights of tankers and fishing fleets laboured, awash in heavy weather. It was a winter seascape, given over to necessity and hard work. The beaches, tatters of their summer festivals streaming in the wind, were rainswept and empty.

Our train had started from Lecce, in the far south, early that morning. By nightfall, it would arrive in Milan. We shared the middle stretch, in a second class compartment, with families of internal emigrants going north in search of work. They were running away from the tyranny of family and local vendetta in the south to the tyranny of corporate business in the north. They had the look of people without illusions, used to surviving anywhere. They were poorly dressed, with cheap pretensions to style, particularly the young single ones, among whom we noticed, indifferently displaying her attributes, a tall, rather beautiful prostitute.

She got down, as we did, at Ancona. We watched her swaying off down the platform with an air of magnificent imperviousness about her, followed by the furtive eyes of dozens of males in the waiting trains. Ancona is a port city – Joyce, who was twice robbed there, had savage words for it – serving Trieste and the Yugoslav coast. She had come north, perhaps, for the passing trade. If not, she would do as we did – dine in the station buffet, and catch the train through the mountains to Rome.

After the austerity of our mountain kitchen, the Ancona buffet seemed like a first class restaurant. In fact, it was nothing out of the ordinary and the starched magnificence of the waiters no more than the due respect, paid everywhere in Italy, to the sacred act of sitting down and eating, albeit on plastic tables and chairs, with the arrivals and departures of trains registering on screens overhead.

Almost nothing going north or south through Ancona came or went on time – we listened in dread for the words *sciopero* (strike) or *guasto* (breakdown, usually during rain). It was a bottleneck for overlapping trains, with crowds surging forward to the doors and windows, ignoring the muffled announcements, asking those already aboard where the train was headed. At least one victim of misapprehension travelled out of Ancona with us, his face pressed against the glass in quiet despair as the train carried him further and further away from his destination. At Falconara we left him behind on the platform, a windswept victim of Italian public transport, the pounding surf behind him, the rain beating in.

We boarded our third train at Foligno, in the middle of the mountains. It was a local train, made up of discarded rolling stock from the principal routes. It moved with nineteenth-century stateliness through the bare vineyards and black November ploughland below Spello and Assisi. On it, besides ourselves, were members of various religious orders, and a bearded Spanish idealist in a Franciscan robe, so lost in his mystical apprehensions he had stayed on a station too far and had to be gently redirected by the conductor, who looked as if he was used to coping, on this line, with spiritual as well as practical contingencies. We had left the rain behind us on the coast. A blast of westering sun transfigured us for a moment – the travellers, the train, the pink outworks and gold windows of Assisi itself – as we rolled on to Perugia. We were three hours north of our village in the Abruzzo. It had taken us a whole day to get here.

Our hostess, an American who had lived in the region for the past ten years, met us at the station. She was running one of the larger language schools in Perugia, a town which in summer has about 25,000 language students at its University for Foreigners, and in winter a big enough catchment area of Italians studying English to keep several schools afloat. She had established herself in a small way before the boom in language teaching, and was now paying off her mortgage on a rambling contadino house at the back of Assisi. She was part of a whole generation of expatriates, English and American, who had settled in central Italy, and were now living vaguely seigniorial lives, with the implicit acquiescence of the locals.

'Your readings and classes,' she told us 'will be packed with foreigners. But don't expect too many Italians.'

There was a large English faculty at the university, she said, but that didn't mean anything. The students, almost exclusively young women who desired entry into the lifelong security of state school jobs, went there only to discover which texts they must learn by rote for the examinations, and to flirt with their examiners in such a way as to ensure success. The lecturers, on the other hand, only went to collect their salaries. As a living wage, these were inadequate, so they concentrated on second jobs elsewhere, and neglected both their students and the literature itself, in which their interest was nil, as we would discover, she said, by their non-attendance at our own sessions.

'You have to realize,' she said sadly, 'this country for all its civilized reputation, cares mainly for money and appearances.'

We saw what she meant by appearances when we walked with her on the Corso Vannuci. It was the hour when the *alto borghese* of Perugia paraded itself before the mirror of its social peers, after stepping collectively out of the shop-windows on either side of the Corso. As a display of arrogant wealth, it reduced the Abruzzo to a chapped indigence. A bitter wind blew down the Corso, and we stepped into the nearest bar. Our hostess mingled with the well-dressed people drinking aperitifs, and exchanged the light social patter demanded of her. In a country run on personal acquaintance and the power of someone's word, it paid to be friendly to everyone. Whatever her private reservations, she was playing by the rules.

Italy is a country of iron social conformity. Because of the anarchic image of its public life, this conformity is not immediately apparent. But at a quotidian level, clothing, food, the etiquette of family and marital life, impose themselves with robotic consistency. It was no surprise, therefore, to emerge at seven to an empty Corso from which the *alto borghese* had vanished, as one person, to their evening meal.

We ate ours in a place off the Corso, with our hostess and some of the young English teachers from her school. They were recent graduates, testing the foreign waters for a while, before returning to Britain to take up careers, most of them, and settle down. Italy, for a year or two, was cheap wine, discotheques, a casual affair, a whiff of freedom. She fussed over them like a mother hen, picking up the tab for them at restaurants, seeing that the frugal accommodation they subsisted in was adequate.

The following afternoon, all the teachers came to the reading. There were many Americans and other resident foreigners, as our host had predicted, and a scattering of local Italians. It was a successful event for which we were handsomely paid, but when it was over, there was less the sense of having communicated something to an audience as of having discharged a social obligation.

Winter had arrived in Umbria. The *tramontana*, a freezing wind off the Apennines, blew down the wind tunnel of the Corso Vanucci. African streetsellers stamped their feet and folded their arms against the cold. A Peruvian couple, busking for college fees, danced and sang Andean songs. Outside the butchers, the wind ruffled the feathers of glossy fowl and tiny iridescent songbirds shot in the hunting season, hanging on hooks in bunches. Workmen were stringing Christmas lights across the principal streets. At night, in the wind, they swayed slightly and shimmered like xylophones.

We stayed for a few days, doing classes, shopping for Christmas, experiencing the perfumeries, the confectionery shops, the jazz clubs. We tried to replenish our stock of books, but found the same thin provender everywhere – a few Penguin Classics for the college market, a shelf of middlebrow novels for the holiday reader. These novels spoke volumes about how the south is perceived – a playground, a garden of convalescence, a fantasy out of E. M. Forster. Here in Umbria, we were part of that fantasy Italy, the axis from Venice to Rome through which millions of visitors funnelled every summer. The novels, shoved to the back of the shop for the time being, would be brought out again in the spring, when the fantasy repeated itself. After the Abruzzo, the beauty of Umbria felt sanitized, tame. We looked out from the high balconies of Perugia over a humanized landscape, mild mountains and plains cradling a middle ground of existence. It breathed moderation and dullness, the conformities of family life. The ruinous battles of the German retreat in the Second World War had passed it by. Now, it was being bypassed by the vivifying heterodoxies of peace. Relative to the rest of Italy, our hostess told us, it was seen as the ideal place to bring up children, to retire to, or to cultivate, in the shadow of the great fresco series on the walls of San Francesco di Assisi, the minor arts, such as sketching and landscape gardening.

At night, through the window of our hotel room, we could see another side of Umbria. Neon factory signs, a disembodied capitalism, blinking on and off in the Tevere valley. Groups of Africans hung around outside the *Quaestura*, their gateway to legitimate residence. Beneath the wealth, the Catholic respectability of Umbria, there was another world, of drugs and Nigerian prostitutes, channelled in through Rome, servicing the night traffic that cruised endlessly through the lit vortex of tunnels below Perugia. We had seen the wads of pornography for sale on the Corso. We had read the molestation headlines in the local papers. The perfectly groomed couples strolling arm in arm, the spoiled children, the giftwrapped chocolates for the family visit each weekend, were only half the story.

'You could stay in Umbria through the winter,' our kind hostess suggested. 'I could find a house for you, if you like.'

It was eleven in the morning. The icy platform of Perugia station, where we were standing, was sprinkled with sawdust. It would be late that night, if not the following day, before we reached our tiny, cold village. Life here was comfortable, a little too comfortable. A few days here had made us realize what the Abruzzo meant to us – the freezing iron of necessity, with real energies flowing through it. We thanked her for everything, and said no.

12

THREE DAYS AFTER OUR RETURN to the village, the snow began in earnest. All autumn, as Stefania had predicted, it had gathered on the peaks. Grey weathers had occluded them, they had emerged into the blue air capped with frosted icing. Our nights had hardened with cold. In the mornings the roadside puddles were frozen over, and everything in the shadows rimed white. Apart from the odd light dusting, however, the snow had held off. Now, in the middle of November, the skies lowered like a roof over the valley, and the snow started falling.

It fell for hours, in the late afternoon and evening, through its own strange luminosity, the heavy flakes falling vertically past our windows, accumulating in inches on the railings, bringing a weightless hush on everything. Outside, we could hear the muffled voice of Gegeto cursing it, as his snow shovel rang on the road, in a mad attempt at clearing a path. At least it seemed mad until I joined a few others gingerly picking their way over the slippery crust to the shop. By the time I got back, the power had failed and the house was in darkness. Soon, the lights blinked on again, but we were to lose them on and off through the evening as snow accumulated on the powerlines and fell off again. It was still snowing heavily after dark, a dramatic curtain of snow sheeting down through the night as it rose to a metre on the ground. Throughout the village, we could hear the muffled whirring of wheels, the futile grinding of engines.

Then it stopped. After a few minutes, the village began to fill with the sound of voices shouting, people out and about, excited by the big change, the occurrence of an event. We found a couple of pairs of mountain boots and clumped out to join them. As is so often the case in Italy, they were shod and clothed in perfect alpine wear already, as if the snowstorm had been arranged to stage a television commercial. But the snow was real enough. It had battened on everything, and the cars parked in the square were vague blobs of ice-cream piled against the walls. The wheelruts were yellow under the harsh light of our only streetlamp. We followed them in a circuit round the village, with the virgin snow in drifts on either side, and the invisible snowpacked silence of the mountains in the darkness beyond. Big, fantastically perfect afterflakes drifted out of the darkness and settled on our sleeves. Galactic symmetries, pure principles of order, even up here in the human twistedness of the village.

It snowed intermittently through the night. We were afraid for the roof of the house, which had collapsed in on itself in places. On days of heavy rain, we had had to position buckets here and there, to catch the drips through the ceiling that warped the forgotten volumes of Mariolatry on the bookshelves. The weight of the snow, we feared, would bring the whole structure down on top of us. Our fears weren't shared by the squirrel in the attic. We could hear him scampering around, lifting and dropping his storage of acorns with a sound like marbles being played. If his instincts told him it was safe up there, we would trust ours down here, and stop dreaming of snowdrifted beds under an open night sky.

We woke to fantastic stillness, intensified light off the ground outside. It was very, very cold. My feet ached on the freezing stone floor and the stone flight of stairs that led to the downstairs bathroom. We had piled everything we had in the way of clothing, coats and blankets on the bed. In the shivering interval between leaving this warm cocoon and getting dressed, we had to stand in front of a lit gas fire. Another gas fire, pulled up as close as possible, was necessary in the kitchen as we boiled coffee. The body heat seemed to drain through our feet into the insatiable stone floors beneath us. The house, pleasantly cool in summer, had become a cold storage unit.

It was warmer outside than in, so we laced up our boots and went out. Long jagged spikes of ice hung like arrested waterfalls from the eaves of the houses. The sky in the valley was a white snow-mist, barely distinguishable from the snow on the ground. A yellow snowplough moved slowly in the direction of the village, churning the road behind it into mush, pushing huge banks of dirty snow to either side. It had worked its way down from Poggio in the small hours, and the road was open now, though freezing. Through this brown slush we waded in the direction of the bridge. Ahead of us clouds of sparrows, and the occasional rare jay driven out of hiding by hunger, pecked at the road, chivvied along, as we were, by the flurries of icy wind that hurt our ears. Under the bridge, weird sculptures of ice sprang from the rocks, between which a channel of water ran darkly, spreading here and there to pools of gelatinous green, in which amazingly, cold-bloodedly, hovered a trout or two.

Back in the village, our post had arrived. Alessandra, wearing black and yellow, was in a mixed frame of mind. Black, because of the cold desolation of her post office, yellow because of the momentary excitement of the first big snow, which allowed her to sport some flamboyant footwear.

'I fought my daughter for these this morning,' she said, pointing to the huge, red fur-lined ski-boots she was wearing. 'I fought her and I won.'

The snow-mist lifted, and a glorious blue calm asserted itself. Even in winter, even in the mountains, the Italian sun had a lenient warmth. We could see across the valley to where the road wound up, beyond Poggio, to the ski resort. It was a line of slow-moving traffic, cars with coloured chains on their wheels and skis strapped to the roofracks. Down on the coast, everyone had had the same idea at once. The winter season had begun.

On Sunday, we borrowed Cesare's car and drove up as far as Poggio. It was even more snowed-in than our own village. Spades had cleared the steps up the steep, narrow alleyways. Crusts of snow higher than a man clung to the walls of the houses. The residents had had to exit through upstairs windows before clearing the drifts covering their front doors. But Poggio, unlike our own village, had an overview of the snow. From its balconies, we looked north at the jagged spine of the Apennine range, a dazzling field of white that hurt our eyes. Winter in its first immaculate state, a pure white crust under a depthless blue, with the dark lines of geologic striations showing through. Whenever the weather cleared, we would have this high, white circle of peaks around us now, all through the winter.

*

Within days, the snow on the roads had cleared and normal traffic resumed. The travelling shop that had maddened and entertained us all summer had found the going too rough and abandoned us for the winter. Instead, a Sicilian merchant rattled into the square twice a week in a truck loaded with gigantic southern oranges and lemons. The summer vegetables were gone, but the big Sicilian fruit crop was now in season. He had an ambiguous weighing scale of a primitive type, and engaged the local women in shouting matches. But his arrival broke the isolation, for apart from him there was only an occasional salt merchant passing through, with his lorryload of rock crystals for breaking ice on the ground, which he sold, from door to door, in two-pound bags.

For a week at a time, the rubbish skip at the end of the village went unemptied. We watched it overflow with our accumulated refuse. Cesare never tired telling us that our plastics, though claimed to be biodegradable, were nothing of the sort. The government commissions set up to establish biodegradability had been a sham, a fraud. What was thrown into the skip – tins, plastic bags, used syringes – would clog up the ecological cycle down the road, he told us. The visual effects, which were to last all winter, were bad enough. What with the dead vegetation and the patches of dirty snow, these scatterings added the final touch of downtroddenness, of wintry desolation, to the village. At night, a starving fox came down from the woods to feed there, at the edge of the circle of light. The big, hungry shepherd dogs scavenged and tore at the refuse bags, while cats looked on, waiting for half a chance. It became a dangerous place to go near, a place of bleakness and savagery.

Through the month of November, we gradually mastered the science of air and fire. At the price of having a knifelike freezing draught in the small of our backs, we could maintain a strong pull of smoke up the chimney. But the blaze, once it got going, made up for everything. On it we roasted the sweet chestnuts we had gathered in the woods in October, and although we didn't have the new harvest wine to go with it, as tradition required, we felt as if Saint Martin himself, whose time of year it was, had reprieved us from the cold.

It is a strange experience to gird yourself in an overcoat and thick mountain boots with heavy socks, when you are going to work in your own house. Yet every morning, after coffee, I ascended the stone stairs with this tonnage of clothing on me, and entered the cold room overlooking the valley. It was the junk room, full of old mattresses and bedsteads – my Freudian couch for daydreams when I tired of sitting at the table I had rigged by the window. Sometimes, in the small hours, when the *tramontana* blew across the dark valley against that exposed corner of the house, I heard a crash as the window blew in and the table overturned, scattering sheets of paper wildly about the floor. It was one step removed from the elements, a cockpit over the valley, a listening post up to which drifted the sounds of the village gossiping, arguing, talking to itself.

In the bitter mornings from November onwards, the window was rimed with frost. Among the junk I unearthed a dilapidated gas fire fitted with a cylinder and found to my amazement and gratitude that it worked. Which is to say it provided, after some minutes' scratching of matches and floating of flame hopefully over the radiator, a small plaque of bluish-yellow heat that wobbled over the mesh before settling into something so gladdening to the heart and senses, such a beneficient filtrate into the cold morning mind, that I am tempted to name it the muse of an entire winter. Without it, I wouldn't have lasted an hour in that frozen junk room. Instead, I pulled it up as close beside me as I could without burning my clothes, rocked quietly back and forth on my chair, and let the harsh smells of escaping gas and burning dust invade my daydream like hashish, until I had entered a tracelike state where the weather no longer mattered.

In this state of heightened attention, the village came back to me as a complex of primary sounds, primary human emotions. Frustration, rage, the grip of necessity. If the village embodied anything, it embodied disappointment, an acute sense of human limitation. Therefore, to overcome this, the villagers were great daydreamers. They dreamed incessantly of making it big in America, despite the disillusioned who had already drifted back from there. Occasionally, they woke to the pain of their actual condition. It was then, outside my window, that the snarling sounds of their arguments, their petty litigations, reached me from below – or not so much reached me as fell into the dark pool of primary receptivity I had become, where anything and everything was reconstituted as language.

> Lost in the fog at four thousand feet
> When the lights come on, I can see them all,
> The mountain villages, so small
> A blind man feels his way about

ON THE SPINE OF ITALY

Without a stick and everyone overhears
Everyone else, as they quarrel and shout,
And still they are all alone –
And the places, the years,
Who redeems them?

As the impressions organized themselves into an approximate musicality, I jotted them abstractedly on to paper and resumed the dreamlike, incantatory rocking, the inner listening, with the heat in the small of my back and the freezing mountain landscape outside. Not even interruptions bothered me, so completely was I living in the present. I even welcomed their incongruities, as the incongruities of reality itself. As far as I was concerned, the Person from Porlock, in the form of a salt merchant or an old lady knocking on the door, was just as likely to be the messenger of grace I needed. Once the process was started, everything was grist to the mill.

This, which in one way seemed like an eternity, went on for no more than the hour or two I could sustain it. In the afternoon I went back up there and resumed the rocking, the listening, the waiting for sounds and rhythms to form themselves into a pattern of words. As often as not, the mechanism jammed and the mind circled pointlessly in a groove of shallow speculation, empty fantasy. Alcohol, that great transporter of the villagers into imaginary paradises, might have loosened my tongue. Instead, I lay on my Freudian mattress and listened a while to rhythmic or discordant music, releasing the body, putting the forebrain to sleep. When the phrases suggested themselves again, I took off the headphones and returned to the table.

I bolt the shutter, bank the fire
And pick up Plato on the Good.
The lumberjack, who gives us wood
For nothing, I see him across at the bar
Where shadows argue, the porkpie hats
Of failures home from Canada, playing skat
And fourhand poker . . .

We were alone with ourselves, as a village, as isolated human beings, in the reduced ambit of winter. Through the dark, cold days of November and December I worked up there, with the perspective which months of living in the village had given me. In that room, in that village, in that winter, I had silence. But more than mere silence, which can be had artificially anywhere, it was a silence in the presence of objects, people, dwellings marked by the pain of particular existence, by the *genius loci*, seething with inarticulate energies. It was a place that had gone unuttered, a place largely bypassed by the world of language and culture, whose only poet, Silone, had left it half a century ago.

Castelli, Cerqueto, cold San Giorgio
Float in the fog, red atmospheres
Connected to each other and to here
Where I link your fate with hers and mine,
Unconsciousness everywhere. Fifty years ago,
In exile, writing Bread and Wine
The War was coming. Now, below your shrine,
Memory tries to wake
Blind monuments, to the Fascist dead,
Disheartened villages, men who cannot shake

ON THE SPINE OF ITALY

The ant of toil from their Sunday clothes,
Slatternly women, old for their years,
The Christian cross, the Communist rose,
With the human word you said.

It wasn't the thing I had come up here to write. But walking around the village after work, in the snow and the darkness, with the glances of mute enquiry upon me and the smells of cooking coming from the small lit windows, it was altogether realer.

13

THERE WAS ALWAYS ENOUGH reality. In December, after a month of fog and mist overhanging the valley, it began to snow heavily again. It was a week before Christmas, and the village already had an exhausted, hypothermic air. Within a few hours, the snow had covered everything. While we lay in bed, we could hear masses of it sliding off the church roof, with a heavy, defecatory thump, into the side passage. I listened to it in the dark, without any sense of romance, aware of the obstacle it would present to my carrying wood next day.

Our first consignment, Silvio's present to us, had dwindled to almost nothing. And his attitude had hardened in the meantime, watching me come and go, which I did with increasing embarrassment, to wheel a barrow full of logs back to the house. I had begun to dread these trips to and from the woodpile, and to wait for moments when the coast seemed clear and I could do my collecting without being overseen by one or other member of the family. But the coast was never clear – there was always someone sunning themselves on a balcony, glancing out of a window, happening by. However casual the contact, however sunny the greeting, I knew my presence at the woodpile was being reported back to Silvio himself. I began to feel like a thief.

Simple arithmetic told me the situation could not continue much longer. What had been, at the end of October, a substantial woodpile, had dwindled to one third of its size in a month. Besides ourselves, it was feeding, all day every day, the stoves of several branches of his family. I had tried, indirectly, to find out if Silvio intended to replenish it. The adolescent Graziano, who ran their little family bar, assured me that any day now Silvio was going into the mountains, when the snow cleared on the roads up there, to bring back a new lorryload. Nothing happened, however, and the next time I went into the bar to find out the situation, I was confronted with a circle of family members drinking in silence around Silvio, who sat brooding on a chair in the middle of the room, staring at nothing. They were clearly waiting for him to make up his mind about the provision of wood for their stoves. He, equally clearly, was sunk in a dark, alcoholic stupor and had been for weeks.

He followed me outside, and gestured at the woodpile. In the brightness of external reality, however desolate it otherwise was, he himself seemed less intimidating, a small pinched man whose eyes expressed, alternately, timidity and violence. He spoke at some length, and in dialect, about the woodpile, and what he said seemed to confirm Graziano's optimism about the arrival of new wood and the availability of the present supply for everyone, including ourselves. On this interpretation, we shook hands and parted. Alas, I had misunderstood him.

The morning after the big snow, matters came to a head. I opened the kitchen door to find a metre of snow in the passage between the house and the woodpile. We could have managed for that day without extra wood, but it if was going to be difficult to wade through the snow today with a wheelbarrow of wood, then judging by the louring sky and the prospect of snowbound days ahead, it was going to be impossible tomorrow. I set off on the ugly errand.

The woodpile itself had disappeared somewhere beneath a huge drift of snow. The yellow, cut ends of a few logs poked tantalizingly out from somewhere near the bottom of the snowdrift. As I began, rather half-heartedly, to work one or two out from the depths of the snow, Silvio appeared, walking unsteadily up from the square to the door of his house. We caught sight of each other at the same instant, and paused. As if by magic, the door to the balcony opened, and the reptilian woman of the house slithered out to watch the impending scene. She was not to be disappointed.

'Wood – finished!' he began massively, fixing me with his eye as one fixes on someone guilty of a great and public stupidity.

'Wood – finished! I told you – no more wood! *Capito? Capisce Italiano?*'

As we stood there, exchanging our few loaded words, various faces dragged themselves to the small windows of surrounding houses. Our falling out would be common knowledge within half an hour. It was an argument about everything and nothing. Nothing in the sense that it was over a few pieces of wood. Everything in the sense that the few pieces of wood were all the village possessed. Now, in the depths of winter, there was no more room for generosity. Behind the minor injustice of the misapprehension he had fostered in us regarding the wood, there was the major injustice of our being there in the first place. We were haves, who had come into a village of have-nots, and we were battening on its limited resources. All this was implicit in our exchange, witnessed by half the village. With the snow,

the wood, the dourness of people and houses in the background, truly it was a scene out of Silone. Whether I liked
it or not, it was I, not he, who was cast in the role of the
villain of the piece.

This, along with the stone-throwing in the autumn, was
one of the few moments the village showed its teeth, and we
felt, however briefly, it might not be possible to stay on up
there. We had been advised against it by many people who
had offered us rooms for the winter down in Teramo – some
who knew the realities of the village and some who, quite
simply, found the idea of living in such a place unimaginable
in any circumstances. In fact the bad moment passed quickly,
like a lanced abscess, slow and painful only in the accumu-
lation of its poisons. A few days later, in the post office, we
met Silvio's tough, unflappable wife.

'Ignore him!' she told us. 'He is saying such things to
everyone at the moment. It's not personal. It's just he is . . .
in a bad way. If he doesn't bring wood soon,' she added,
'myself and the children will move down to Montorio, to my
parents' house.'

That was the end of the wood episode. It left us, more
acutely than the sound of water being siphoned off, with a
sense of the poverty of the village and the fine, invisible web
of its property relations. But it left no residue, except the
immediate problem of how to heat our house. We turned
our attention to the stove.

The priest had always insisted on the stove. Once we got the
stove going, he said, our troubles for the winter would be
over. Padre Simone would come over from his mountain
village to the north, and show us the workings of the

stove. He did in fact come over one day, when we were out. He mustn't have stayed long. He seemed always to have been a shadowy presence in the village, even when actually living there.

He had, however, been the only living expert on this particular stove, the workings of which frustrated the best efforts of half the village. Before winter arrived, we had effectively given up on it. It was a big black stove, propped against one wall of that cold-floored ecclesiastical parlour we had avoided using so far, except to pass through on the way to the kitchen. It had a black, crooked flue, broken and bandaged at every joint, that ran up the wall through the ceiling, through our bedroom, and on up to the roof. It was fuelled on kerosene, of which there was a supply under the stairs. It stood there like a Sphinx, setting us the riddle.

The priest had asked the local handymen, Gegeto and Carlo, to take it outside, dismantle it, and reassemble it in working order. Wisely, they didn't refuse this impossible task outright, but in polite fashion procrastinated until it had been forgotten. They were understandably in no mood to make a public laughing stock of themselves. They took the view that, in this case, surgery would be fatal. If it was moved, it would never function again. Anyway it was an old model, they said, for which parts were no longer available. Better to scrap it altogether, and buy a new one.

In principle, it was a simple mechanism. You poured kerosene into a small tank. It filtered through a pipe to the stove proper, where it fuelled six little jets of flame whose effluent went off up the chimney, while the black mass of the stove radiated heat into the room. To open or close the kerosene inflow, you turned a manual regulator. But no kerosene was filtering through. Either there was a blockage in the pipe or the manual control wasn't working. In either case, finding the fault could be like finding a needle in a haystack. Meanwhile, we had run out of wood, it was the middle of winter, and the temperature outside was below zero.

A day after the wood episode, by sheer accident, we cracked the code. We discovered that the manual regulator, while turning all too easily of itself, wasn't turning the shaft that actually opened the flow. The connection between the two had been broken. So we removed the knob and turned the shaft itself with pliers. The effect was immediate and dramatic. This time, when we dropped a lighted piece of cotton wool soaked in alcohol into the stove, instead of the blue flame dwindling to extinction as it had done countless times before, it strengthened and turned yellow as it made contact with the kerosene outflow points. Within minutes, the inside was a mass of white flame, and the stove had begun to give off heat.

To say this transformed our situation would be an understatement. Never was the acrid smell of kerosene so welcome about the place, nor the wash of white flames when we lifted the lid of the stove so delicious. The heat restored the point of central repose our lives had been lacking up there since the onset of winter. As it emanated from the stove, we began to see the cold parlour, with its glass-topped table and tasteless decorations, in a different light. Now it seemed a haven of warmth and comfort, the true centre of the house, and we cast the kitchen into outer darkness, at least until the spring. That very night, we began to eat our meals in the parlour, and our single armchair we manoeuvred down the stone stairs from the bedroom, positioned it on one side of the stove, with the most comfortable of the plain chairs on the other, and settled down to survey winter in the village from a standpoint of reasonable independence.

After the initial breakthrough, we never again had a problem with the stove. Every afternoon about four, when the light began to fail and the temperature in the mountains to plummet, we dropped in a piece of lit wadding and the thing sprang to life with companionable mutterings and grumblings. By midnight, when it was far below zero outside, not only were we ourselves and the surviving green dumbledores warm, but the bedroom immediately overhead that awaited us was too.

The village, in its small way, was preparing for Christmas. The shop had introduced a freezer, full of packaged vegetables, hamburgers, french fries and fish fingers, to internationalize the local cuisine. It had a glass display case, containing cheeses and cold cuts of meat, clinically administered by the women in starched white. The *co-operativa*, as it stood now, would have done justice to a hospital.

They had introduced a small stand of Christmas gifts and confectionery, a smaller and far poorer version of the extravaganzas we had witnessed in Perugia. There were bottles of Spumante and Amaro, the bitter *digestivo* favoured in the Abruzzo. There were sundry mechanical toys, timed to autodestruct a week after they had been bought. And there was a big assortment of giftwrapped *panettones*, the soft fruity cakes filled with jam or chocolate that symbolize the Christmas season in Italy. We bought some for Silvio's family, as a fence-mending gesture.

In the bar, the men played cards obsessively. The lights were on until two in the morning, as they engaged in gigantic poker sessions. As it was Christmas, they were betting heavily and playing for real stakes. We knew villagers who had been literally ruined, dispossessed of their property and the shirts off their backs, by such sessions. The late night shouting and roaring across the road had plenty of reality behind it. But anything, especially in winter, was better than boredom, and cards were the one thing in the lives of the village men that lifted the burden of empty time off their backs.

A week before Christmas, a truck arrived from the commune of Poggio, with a string of coloured lights. In the course of one dark afternoon, they were draped over the solitary pine in the piazza. In the evening, switched on, it became our communal Christmas tree. Meanwhile, in the church, Gegeto had constructed a huge elaborate crib out of moss and mountain rocks – a minature landscape threaded with electric lights, through which wandered shepherds, wise kings and animals, in the direction of the Holy Family. Until Christmas night, this massive construction went unwitnessed by almost everyone in the village. After Christmas, it was almost immediately dismantled. It was a labour of love. The lights on the pine tree, which were the work of the state, were still there the following May.

These were dark, cold days in the village. The temperature hardly rose above freezing, and the dirty snow hardened on the ground. It was the low ebb of the year, the time of solstice. But it was good for one thing at least – the killing of local pigs.

Gianbattista, a small man with permanent bristle on his

face, kept a pig in a wretched sty below the paddock where the horses were watered. We passed it every day on our walk around the back of the village – a few planks nailed together, with that heavy unmistakable smell emanating through them, and the occasional low belch from the pig inside, contentedly unaware that its dwelling place was the porcine equivalent of Death Row. Giambattista had decided to wait until the raw, cold days around Christmas, when all the flies were dead and there was no danger of them laying eggs in the meat and contaminating it. Now, it seemed, the time was right.

Although we were in our house at the time, it was clear throughout the village that the pig had struggled and died a slow, terrible death, roped in on all sides though it had been. A kind of bestial curiosity had dragged a large number of villagers down to the scene. We heard shots at irregular intervals, punctuated by the weird screaming of the pig in its death agony, now short, now long, mind-shredding sounds that permeated the village. Eventually, after the best part of an hour, a silence ensued.

The following day, we passed the scene of the struggle. The mud in front of the sty had been churned into a red porridge, a slick of blood oozing away into the ditch. For yards around, the snow was a dark red stain. Despite the cold the smell of blood hung in the air. There were buckets of it everywhere. The pig itself, a profane crucifixion, had been hung up on a gibbet to be dismembered. Opened, disembowelled, it was so big that Giambattista and another villager, fortifying themselves with slugs of rough red wine from a flagon, were going at it with axes, to smash the vertebral column.

'Wait until after Christmas!' he called to us. 'Sausages for everyone!'

Wood, vegetables, meat. If times had been kind to them, the villagers in their turn were generous with their good luck. If it had not, they were not. There was no middle ground. In the village, it was either a feast or a famine.

14

ON CHRISTMAS EVE, ALESSANDRA and her husband Stefano drove over to collect us in the large Land Rover he used for part of his duties. Between himself and the priest, we had found ourselves being driven out of the village – always a very public moment, when everyone stops to watch – by a variety of vehicles representing church and state, neither held in high esteem in these parts. Thankfully, our shotgun wedding with the forces of authority was not held against us. In its gruff, taciturn way, the village had taken us to heart. We knew we were admired for wintering up there, for sharing the hardships of the place, even if our reasons for doing so were not understood.

Alessandra, for the occasion, was extravagantly dressed. She had always badmouthed the village women, especially the younger ones, for their masculine swagger in jeans and heavy shoes, or for succumbing too completely to maternal dullness in their dress, or for wrapping themselves in widow's weeds before their time. This was unfair. As a state representative, she was financially a cut above the rest, and they resented her for it. Only her friend Stefania, she was fond of saying, knew how to dress herself as a woman should. On this occasion, she was modelling an extraordinary mink coat, a present to her from Stefano. With childish vanity, she revealed that the pelts of fifty mink had gone into the making of it – it was possible to see them, one against the other, in the grain of the coat. She looked like a walking fur-trapper in it, and we remembered the existence of Stefano's mink farm higher in the mountains. As if to underline the implications, as we drove past the rubbish skip on the way out of the village, our lights caught the fiery red brush of a fox's tail disappearing into the darkness.

Stefano, after fifteen years of marriage, was still a good-looking man. He treated his wife with affection and detachment. His safety valve was the bar in Prato – it seemed to be the key to his survival in the married state, this capacity of his to insulate a part of himself from the currents of warm irrationality that submerged him at home. By this stage, we had heard both sides of their story – Alessandra's fits of blind jealousy, his own wry observations on the stamina required to sustain a lifelong relationship. As students of marriage ourselves, we took a close interest in all this, reciprocated by Alessandra in the form of intimate anatomical enquiries directed at me, and intermittent pokings in my wife's pelvic region.

'Ah, marriage is one thing,' she sighed. 'But only when children arrive does the real struggle begin.'

Their own two children greeted us in the most open, affectionate way, as those who expect nothing but good of the world and have yet to be disappointed can only do. There is a degree of intimacy in Italian socializing which is almost but not quite sexual, and testifies to the unconscious sophistication with which people interact. So, in this conservative Abruzzese family, when the beautiful teenage daughter artlessly laid her head against the inside of my knee as we sat by the fire – stoked, as usual, by the old woman in black – I had the wit to take it as less of a compliment than I might have further north. Whatever problems these children would meet in later life, sexual adjustment wouldn't be one of them.

Presents were opened – mountain socks for me, Chinese slippers for my wife, a loud diamond-patterned sweater for Stefano. We ate fish, the traditional Christmas Eve dish in Italy. All this while, people drifted in and out. The front door of the apartment had an exhausted look to it from the number of openings and closing it had endured. Even in winter, the children lived half their lives on the street outside, and were constantly putting on and taking off their snowboots. There were adult visitors too, people from the village who had come to greet us. And there was a woman doctor, a friend of Alessandra who was spending the night. She lived alone in a hospital room in Teramo. She had come from Greece years ago as a medical student, poured all her energies into becoming a doctor in Italy – difficult for a woman even now – and having achieved this status, collapsed into the exhaustion of middle age. Her tired, intelligent face looked wordlessly at us as we ate. Then she went off with Alessandra to give her one of the many mysterious injections she took, before reappearing, after an indeterminate period, to clear the table and mop the floor.

Having eaten, Stefano retired to the sofa with his *Gazzetto dello Sport* and his remote control. It being Christmas, the TV programmes were even more atrocious than usual. We watched a bumper edition of a women's show, hosted by a big, raucous, sufficiently sexy but maternally curved woman named Rafaella, who harangued a captive audience of younger women dressed in white. All of them, it seemed, were programmed to break into hysterical enthusiasm at the mention of babies – particularly the vaguest hint, dropped by Raffaella herself, that she might be expecting one – or to cluster around spoiled children brought to the microphone as some beardless wonder crooned a ballad. There was a male heart-throb contest, in which four exceptionally nondescript individuals were judged by viewers calling in. Naturally, the most anaemic specimen won hands down. Other diversions included a young woman in bunny costume speaking babytalk to children who phoned in, and the inevitable gambling wheel in the background, to fill up lacunae, until Raffaella reappeared, holding a baby in her arms, and on cue, the young women in white erupted hysterically again. Mussolini himself couldn't have devised a purer piece of cultural fascism. Alessandra, pushing her mop around the floor, loved it.

Towards midnight we set off again, through the mountains, to our own village. It was a night of Wordsworthian magnificence. The skies had cleared and a full moon lit the pristine snow of the peaks, below which glittered the warm cluster of lights that was Poggio, and a little further down, the lights of our own village, wavering slightly in the distance across the valley. According to Stefano, it had been a remarkably mild winter by Abruzzo standards, and if it continued we would, within the month, see the first wild flowers of spring come into bloom. Despite the clarity of the night, though, the air outside was still piercingly cold. The mountain road was icy, banked with frozen snow.

The village square, at midnight, was sheeted in ice. Alessandra, tricked out in high heels, picked her way to the church entrance on the arm of her husband. The villagers, as they entered the church, wished each other and us an

115

understated Merry Christmas. They had put aside their antipathy to the place for now. They were prepared to listen.

The church, normally an empty freezing shell, was a blaze of lights and fresh flowers. The sceptics, the atheists, the once-a-year men and women and the religious fanatics crowded into the warmed space between four gas fires. Immediately behind us, between his wife and children, Silvio sat and stared catatonically in front of him. At the back of the church, in a group, stood the women who ran the *co-operativa*. They had closed the bar just before Mass, and would open it again afterwards. Old Emilio, who had wheeled babies through the autumn was there. Cesare and Franca were there, carrying their sleeping children in their arms. Stefania, with a bright blue rinse and butterfly stockings, stood stiffly among the old women in black. The man who siphoned water from our house for his horses stood at the back, and various younger men, Nello and Gianfranco, who worked on the tunnel, looked in. It was a rare and ephemeral moment of togetherness in the village.

As the Mass proceeded, various adolescents wandered up the side aisles for a look. Coolly curious, stripped of religious awe, they were the first post-Christian generation in the village. The priest eyed them uneasily as they came and went, gunning their motorbikes outside the church, drowning out his words. Now and again he interrupted himself, with an air of great restraint, and invited them to sit on the front benches.

There were already children on the front benches. They had made their First Communion earlier in the autumn. Out of residual loyalty, they put in a few appearances in the church, annoying the priest by their chatter and mutual amusement as he conducted the service. Now, before his own sermon, he turned to them with a benevolent, fatherly look on his face.

'What is Christmas?' he asked them.

There was a silence, punctuated by embarrassed giggles, as they looked at one another.

'What is Christmas?' he repeated, a little more sharply. 'The birth of—'

'Christ,' said the altar boy Domenico, from behind the priest. Domenico was the son of Michele, a quite exceptionally obsequious man, with a saccharine manner, who danced attendance on the priest over coffee, after his Sunday Masses.

'Exactly, Domenico. Christ. And who was Christ, Domenico?'

A silence.

'Who was Christ anyone?' said the priest, opening the question to the whole congregation.

People shuffled their feet, looked at the ground. There was nothing, he had told us, that annoyed him more than this stony absence of response on the part of the villagers. Grim-faced, he left it at that and went on to the sermon.

But the sermon didn't help either. Did they not realize, he asked them, that the church was there not just on Christmas week, but every week of the year? What kind of example were they themselves, the members of the church of Saint Peter in Rome, giving to their own children, as they staggered around in a state of drunkenness, distributed drugs and made a travesty of sexual morality? Were they not aware of the bad name they had incurred in neighbouring villages? Once more, he wanted to remind them, the church was always there, always ready to forgive the truly repentant –

but if they didn't come to it, what hope was there for them? And now he wanted them to rise with him, and sing out loud and fearlessly.

They rose – all except Silvio, who continued to stare fixedly ahead of him – but they sang neither loud nor fearlessly. They didn't sing at all. Instead, the choral voice-box at the back of the church, primed by Gegeto, sang loud and fearlessly for them, along with the priest. Mutely, we gave each other the hand of peace, mutely the communicants filed up for communion. The muteness, the reserve, was never broken. On the one occasion in the year when he had the ear of the village, he had not gotten through to them.

In fairness, he was desperately tired. His face, over the coffee we boiled for him afterwards, was a haggard sleepless mask. He had worked himself to the point of exhaustion in the weeks before Christmas. Now he had to drive on up to Poggio where another congregation was waiting for him to celebrate its Midnight Mass. After that, in the small hours, he would drive back to Teramo for two hours' sleep before starting his chain of Christmas morning Masses, including another here in the village, after which we would accompany him to the ski resort above Poggio, where his whole family was booked in for the holiday.

After he had gone, we went across to the bar for a drink. The villagers, after a brief after-Mass frenzy, had gone back to their houses. The *co-operativa* was closing for the holiday period, and the women were cleaning the counters, upending chairs on tables and mopping the floors. Their knitting and sewing, the Penelope's loom into which they had woven the tedium of autumn and winter up here, lay on the windowsill, to be taken up in the New Year. Were we going anywhere for the New Year, they wanted to know. Yes, we were going to Bologna. They didn't know Bologna, but they knew Rimini, on the coast near Bologna. We all poured ourselves a drink on the house, and toasted Christmas and the New Year. We all felt we deserved it.

Outside, a fabulous quiet had settled over the village, except for the restless sound of horses in the lower pasture, and away in the frozen woods above us somewhere, the hooting of an owl. In this fabulous silence, the humanity of the village had gone to sleep, with or without its dream of redemption. In the icebound square, the lights on the pine tree flickered noiselessly on and off. White, ill-fed, apparitional, the local sheepdogs roamed from skip to rubbish skip. Above this mixed scene of squalor and homeliness hovered the deep black of infinite space, clarified by altitude and winter, in which the galaxies stood out against a light dusting of supernovae. We worked our way by deduction to the pole star, a tiny remote dot in a cluster of stars. I remembered Plato's Spindle of Necessity, which passes like an axis through the earth from the polestar, wherever you view it from. If we had to spin on that particular axis, then the village was as necessitous a place as any to do it from.

15 IF NECESSITY WAS THE HALLMARK of the village, luxury was the hallmark of the ski resort we drove to on Christmas Day. Here, an entirely different concept of the mountains prevailed – as playground, romantic backdrop and vanity fair. We had rarely been up there, largely for lack of transport. In the autumn, it was out of season, a place of yellowing beechwoods, empty hotels and deserted chairlifts, a few shops selling souvenirs and ski equipment, a few discotheques and pizzerias, all closed. These were arranged around a huge tarmacadamed car park for the miles of traffic that wound up there once the season started. Off season, apart from shepherds driving their flocks through, only a skeleton staff stayed on in the lobbies of the hotels, and behind the counters of coffee shops. By Christmas Day, however, all that had changed.

The snow by the roadside was banked to a height of more than a metre. Fresh snowfalls had rounded out the drifts, and the road was a dry yellow crust where the wheels bit easily, except in the shade. There was a light traffic of people driving back up for lunch, who had spent the morning in Poggio. The rest of Italy had stayed at home, on the traditional family holiday. The day after, it would take to the roads, en masse.

Up north, in the Dolomites, it had been a disastrous season. Snow had not fallen, and the slopes were green at ten

120

thousand feet. The sprinklers were out, whitening the ski runs with artificial snow. Here in the Abruzzo, however, the real thing had fallen. Within a day, this place would be a focal point for the entire Italian jet set. Advance members of that species were already in evidence, as we parked the car in front of the hotel. In the surrounding woods, the chalets were occupied. There were queues at the coffee bars. Between now and the New Year, a great deal of money would change hands up here.

Even the priest, redolent of aftershave, garbed in designer clerical wear, had to stare in awe. Among certain classes of people, it seems that the ugliness of the human body is in inverse proportion to its sartorial pretensions. Certainly this was true of the people we were looking at now – bald, pot-bellied men dressed in skin-tight ski-suits of a bright banana colour; ugly women waddling about like moonwalkers, in oversized fur boots. Even the cars manifested their self-preoccupation in the attention-grabbing colours of their snowchains. A few had been pulled over to one side by the local carabinieri, who were taking out their boredom in random roadchecks. But the pickings were thin. It was, after all, lunchtime on Christmas Day.

The priest announced himself in the lobby of the hotel. He was well known here, where he sometimes said Mass. Unlike the villages, however, where he was met with a certain reserve, here all was deference. His social prestige was recognized and ministered to. And were his family here, he asked. They were indeed, padre, the proprietor smiled. They were waiting upstairs, for him and his guests. The reserved dining room was ready. The cooks were at work on the meal.

'You have come a long way, Gian Piero,' the priest said, 'since your days up here as a *pastore*.'

The proprietor agreed that the business was going well.

Most of the family had arrived the previous night, from the various parts of Italy where they lived. They were already betraying signs of cabin fever as they lolled around on the soft furnishings of the annexe to the private dining room. It had become their habit, as a family, to get together in the mountain resort for a few days over Christmas every year. The men were conservatively dressed, the women tastefully flamboyant, fitted out by couturiers, with their hair styled. They bore traces of former prettiness, even extinguished beauty, of a kind that suggested they had once been chosen for their looks. Now they chased after their spoilt, self-absorbed children, in whom their lives were centred, while their menfolk sat back, fondling gold watches on fobs from inside their Armani cardigans, and discussed higher matters. This, the family of the priest, was of the Italian *alto borghese*. Its ground rules were readily apparent, even to outsiders like ourselves.

They rose in unison to greet us. One or two of them we had met before, and there were others who had yet not arrived. But the majority were unknown to us – the priest's several brothers and their host of chattering wives, the children, the mooning adolescents being sculpted for middle-class respectability, and a nucleus formed by the priest's uncle Fabio, his father, and his handsome formidable mother.

Uncle Fabio asked us about our lives and activities in the village. He was gentle and courteous, but his eyes were sharply particular and intelligent. This was not the village.

There was no evading his questions. So we gave him an exact account of how our days passed there, and what we were writing. He took it all in, giving us his full attention. He worked as a judge in Florence, and was very well read. He had had a difficult time in the courts further north in the Alto Adige, during the period of separatist terror there in the Seventies, when politicals who had planted bombs were being tried, and judges were threatened. Now, in late middle age, life in Florence was quieter. He was part of the eminent inner circle of judges who controlled the legal life of Italy, and he trvelled often to Rome for its meetings. Strangely, for all his sophistication, he had never been outside Italy. Nor had he any wish to go, he told us. Life here was entirely satisfactory, it contented one at every level. In this, he was at one with the priest, and with large numbers of other educated Italians. It seemed only the poor left, and they had their own reasons.

The priest assumed his place at the dining table, where the family was waiting for him to say grace. Immediately afterwards, the wines were uncorked and the waiters began moving from person to person with the first in a long succession of dishes. It was a noisy meal, dominated by the children's end of the table, and punctuated by hugs, kisses, explosions of affection and a quite extraordinary restlessness on everybody's part. I doubt if a single conversation got finished before it was interrupted by expostulations of welcome for some new relative who had wandered in late, or by attempts to placate a crying child by smothering it with kisses. In this good-humoured chaos the meal took place. The antipasti of sturgeon's roe, the creamy pasta, the trays of roast meat were passed around, and the level sank in the bottles of Veneto wine. By the time of the desserts and spumantes, the right level of visceral oneness had been achieved. We were all, friends and relatives, well and truly, '*insieme*'. This condition of being '*insieme*' was, as always, an essentially non-verbal one. We were none the wiser, as analytic entities, about each others' lives, but that wasn't what mattered. It was something else, some integument of Italian togetherness, that had been re-affirmed. It was this primordial, essentially familial thing that made life anywhere else but in Italy so difficult for its sons and daughters.

'But you know,' Uncle Fabio sighed, 'it is this, in a way, that has given rise to the Mafia, to the brutality of the south. This overemphasis on family loyalty, as a substitute for everything else . . .'

A child stood up and recited a poem for the occasion. Everyone clapped. Someone made a speech in honour of one of the priest's younger brothers, a quiet man who worked in finance and whose wife was pregnant, after a miscarriage, with a quick successor to two previous children. She had suffered, the priest said approvingly, but she went on trying to have more. This brother and his wife were making the supreme sacrifice of leaving Italy and going to work, as members of a lay religious circle, in a working-class suburb of Dresden, where they knew no one. Certain contacts would be made for them, and the idea was that they would form the nucleus of a religious group there that would be self-sufficient when they moved on. All this already existed in many parts of Europe, a kind of freemasonry the priest and his family were part of. Now, he was being blessed on his way by priest and family. He would be spreading the idea, their idea, the way of life they were celebrating around this very table.

It was late afternoon when we rose from the table. The priest went to celebrate yet another Mass, this time at an improvised chapel in the ski resort. The rest retired to various rooms, while we put on overshoes and went outside for a walk, before it got dark.

The resort was wide open commercially. All the suffering of the mountains had been refined up here to an aesthetic experience of lit boutiques, the minimalist decor of fast-food emporia. It was a place designed for the moment, where the sports shops angled for the impulse buyer of expensive superfluities, and the rough wooden booths with their rustic tables bore the brunt of a high turnover of quick eaters feeding the cash registers. When the moment passed, this place would return to the deathly silence of closed hotels and empty car parks, with the banished *genius loci* looking on from the woods beyond, at a desecrated space.

Midwinter dusk and the lights of the resort had lent a bluish tinge to the snow on the *pistes*. They sloped up to the grey eminence of Mussolini's ruined lookout on the ridge above. Beyond were the peaks of the Gran Sasso, already shrouded in fresh snowstorms. The *pistes* themselves were strung with lights and threaded with chairlifts. We watched the disappearing shapes of skiers chained into bucket-seats moving up, and the empty seats coming back down. At the top of the *pistes*, the skiers were black dots zigzagging against the lit snow, their shapes enlarging as they swerved downhill towards us through the marker poles, and slewed to a halt in front of us, full size again, their breath coming in gouts of steam against the cold. They were athletes, like those we had seen on Mediterranean amphorae. But unlike the Greeks of old, they were athletes without philosophy.

We saw no one from the village, not even Stefania whose pizzeria was dark and closed. She had gone to Florence, to be with her mother, leaving her husband to fend for himself in the house. One or two of the younger villagers might come to the disco, whose blue neon sign winked on and off against the snow. But apart from exceptions, this was not a world the village had any connection with, either mentally or financially. It belonged to the middle classes of Italy, taking their *settimana bianca*, to the dolce vita of young bodies at play. We breathed its cold mountain air, an ozone of health and artificiality.

Back at the hotel, an argument was in progress. After twenty-four hours cooped up in the hotel, the family were feeling restless and in need of setting off to visit other relatives on the coast. The priest, grey with exhaustion, was awaiting the outcome of deliberations about who would go where in which car. He was being appealed to, by his mother, as the ultimate arbiter and organizer. But he hadn't the energy to organize it. He hardly had the energy to speak. With relief, he pointed to us as his excuse, and made his escape in the car.

There was little traffic on the frozen road, as we drove slowly down. A few wild birds, driven by hunger to peck at the icy yellow crust, flew away as our headlights hit them. Below us, the villages were parcels of light against the deeper darkness of the mountains. Poggio was deserted, a harshness of streetlights on rutted snow. Two miles further down, we crossed the bridge into our own village.

'One thing I have never understood,' the priest said irritably, 'is why, sometime in the past, someone decided to build a house in this place of all places. Then another was built beside it. And another. And another. Why here of all places?'

He had never concealed his dislike for this place. And it was true, you entered a nondescript village, its houses built higgledy-piggledy around a church and a tiny, sloping square, the whole thing perched on a barren promontory that looked likely to crumble away entirely at the next earthquake. There it was, without rhyme or reason, its wild dogs foraging in the bins, its absurd string of Christmas lights winking faintly on the dirty snow in the square. You came back into it from other, better places, with a sense of its wretchedness and squalor, its glaring, heretical pride in its own indignity. And yet, though we didn't say so to the priest, it was more real than the pleasure ground we had just come from. It belonged to the mountains as the other place never would. It was linked to them by a history of human suffering.

16

AT ELEVEN THE FOLLOWING morning, the priest collected us. He was driving us down to Teramo, where we would make our own connections to Bologna. He must have taken a sleeping draught, or something strong enough to wipe out the tensions of his Advent duties, for he was in high good form. He could hardly sit still while we gulped down a coffee, but he was out and about greeting people, across at the bar ordering coffees for everyone. He was a man who lived on his nerves.

All Italy was on the roads. A long line of traffic inched upwards towards the ski resort. It would be afternoon and failing light before they got where they were going. But there they were, bumper to bumper, their tyres grinding and slipping up the icy road, some with chains and some without. As pleasure, it left a lot to be desired. We, on the other hand, glided effortlessly downhill on the free side of the road, the priest saluting every second car that contained someone or other he knew. At a particularly treacherous bend further down, he could bear it no longer. The black ice had slewed chainless cars over to one side. Others tried to squeeze past them and created new blockages in their turn. There were lorries and buses entering the mix at the lower end, and the priest jumped out to direct it, leaving me to guide the car gently down in the wake of his gesticulating. He was alternately traffic policeman, mechanic and friend to the afflicted motorist. A hundred yards further down, I pulled in to the side, and waited for him to tire of his benevolence. Twenty minutes later, he came running down-hill to rejoin us and take the driving seat.

'I must warn them further down,' he panted, 'of the need for chains.'

He left us at the house of Christian and Patricia. Christian was a retired accountant, Patricia a retired schoolteacher. Both had magnificent heads of silvery hair. They lived in an apartment that combined elegance with a sense of arrested time. Double-glazed windows cut out the contemporary buzz of Teramo traffic outside. Their two sons had moved away and they lived quietly – which is to say she chattered endlessly while he interjected the occasional saintly remon-strance. They were both deeply involved in Catholic lay work. He, for a lay person, had risen to the unusual eminence of being ordained a deacon. Even now, in his sixties and after a heart attack, his duties took him all over the Abruzzo on weekends. Of their two sons, one worked with an Italian publishing firm in New York, and the other was a consultant in a Florence hospital. This other, Anselmo, had come back with his wife – rather reluctantly, we sensed – to be with his parents over Christmas. With these two, Christian and Patricia, we sat down to our third big meal in as many days.

At the saying of the grace, it was clear that Anselmo's religious views were not those of his parents. He had the same shock of hair his mother had, but his radiated secular intelligence while hers radiated Catholic fervour. They were a volatile combination, with Christian as uneasy peacemaker. As we bent to our plates around the circular table, we had the feeling of staring into the crater of an extinct volcano in which lay the ashes of many a religious argument. The other son, unmarried, had broken out of this orthodoxy to go and live in New York. His mother still hung tearfully on the other end of long telephone conversations with him. How on earth could he manage over there without her? Anselmo and his wife had made their distance by living in Florence. But, like a good mother, she was selling up here shortly and going to live in Florence too, to be near them. Yes, having children had its difficulties, she told us all over the meal, but it was always worth it.

'And you two,' she said, addressing us, but indirectly getting at the childless Anselmo, 'why do you not have children? Don't you know it's in God's plan for *all* married couples to have children?'

During this one-way flow of conversation, Anselmo and his wife maintained a dignified silence, interjecting only the odd noncommittal remark. Later, as he drove us across the coastal plain to the railway station, he told us how necessary it had been for him to move out of the Abruzzo if he wished a life of his own. Yes, he said, the south was not as bad as it had once been. Since the war, money had come into the Abruzzo and brought with it at least superficial changes, albeit in the worst possible taste. We could see the ugly supermarkets, couldn't we, and the marriage boutiques, their windows filled with the whipped cream of nuptial confections, and the ruined *contadino* houses? But underneath, he insisted, the south was still the south. Your every move was noted – to live as you wished, you needed the anonymity of the big cities further north.

We had made a good choice, he said, in going to Bologna.

*

We arrived late at night. A freezing fog mantled the streets outside the station, and muffled the sounds of passing traffic. Indistinct signs, in blue and yellow neon, advertised hotels across the road. African immigrants stood around in groups, and the times of trains for all the ends of Europe lit up the automatic schedule in the lobby. We were in the industrial north.

To one side, a large marble plaque commemorated the victims of the 1980 station bombing, a *cause célèbre* in Italy. Originally, our friend Franco had told us, it had been ascribed to the left-wing Red Brigade. Later, it had become clear that elements of the fascist black sector in the Italian government had ordered it to be carried out as a diversionary tactic, drawing attention away from other scandals and putting the blame on the communists. Bologna had been chosen, he said, because of its reputation as an independent city within Italy, and its long communist tradition. It was different from everywhere else, he said. It was the most open city in Italy. The rest of Italy was envious and suspicious of Bologna.

We booked into a modern hotel on the Via Indpendenza, and neither of us had ever before been so grateful for the anonymous comforts of hotel existence – the limitless flow of warm ducted air, the carpet of standard hessian, and the white cubic space of the bathroom unit, with its sachets of perfume and soap, and its big silver showerhead gushing hot water. Our faces in the mirrors were burnt and brown, our hair was wild. We looked at ourselves in that padded cell, with its multi-channel TV and its drinks cabinet, and saw the difference between luxury and necessity.

There are cities, like Paris or San Francisco, whose names

are associated with earthly perfection. In its own smaller way, Bologna is one of these. It is a perfection comprised of intellectual and physical elements, with the pleasure principle as the link factor. This blend of intellect, sexual tension, architecture, food and emotional yearning imparts a kind of solidity, a multi-dimensional density to life in these places that is greater in degree than elsewhere. They are described as having a beautiful lifestyle, as if the gap between necessity and the ideal had been closed, and the need for art or religion, which closes this gap, had been replaced by the perfect, integral wholeness of daily life. In the case of Bologna its more sceptical sons, like Pier Paolo Pasolini, have questioned the basis of this apparent perfection, which manages to be both communist and extravagantly, abundantly capitalist at the same time. The answer in Bologna's case, perhaps, lay outside the old centre, in the miles of working-class suburbs whose lights we had seen the previous night on the train coming in – a bit like Plato's philosophical republic, where the slaves are never mentioned.

For three days, we soaked up whatever it is the essence of Bologna consists of. We sat and strolled, drank coffee and read newspapers. We travelled as far away as Venice and Trieste. We were part of the migratory mainstream of northern Europe – the Romany gypsies, the Slav women in headscarves at the stations. The whole of northern Italy was shrouded in winter fog, with magnificent blue intervals when the sun broke through the mists, transfiguring the red and yellow buildings of Bologna, its miles of arcades, and wafting light over the vast, pigeon-filled square in front of the cathedral. The streets emptied at one and filled again at four, when mobs in black leather from the suburbs surged up the Via Independenza and back down again, with a fierce, suppressed rage, like an undercurrent. It was a life thickly textured with history and politics, a far cry from the stark landscapes, the metaphysical absolutes we had left behind us in the Abruzzo.

On New Year's Eve, crowds packed the cathedral square. Arc lights roamed the darkness, settling on the red façade of the City Hall and its big clock face ticking towards midnight. A huge straw effigy of Father Time stood in front of it, awaiting immolation. High over the crowd, two tightrope artists, the Old Year and the New, wobbled towards each other, edged around each other and continued to windows at opposite ends of the square. In a carousel, an orchestra played waltzes, and a ball was in progress in the City Hall. The invitees to the ball were hanging out of the windows in their evening wear, clutching bottles of foaming spumante. As the gold hands of the clock touched twelve, the square exploded in a sea of balloons. Father Time went up in a whoosh of white flame, and collapsed within minutes. Immediately, fizzing and gushing off the battlements of the City Hall, a firework display of monumental proportions whited, blued and incarnadined the darkness with dull pocks of explosion, until the air of the square itself was blue with gunpowder haze and littered with incendiary fallout. Wealthy, respectable men and women dropped firecrackers surreptitiously under each other's feet, and the ground was jumping with little flashes. Various privately operated fireworks whizzed about indiscriminately above the ducking heads of the crowd. We fought our way out of all this, over burst balloons and broken bottles and back down the Via Independenza towards the hotel. Sirens and klaxons raised an operatic wail above the city. Gangs of leatherjacketed youths raced through the arcades. It would go on like this all night. Energies were being released here, the energies of history, of change for better or worse. Here in Bologna, the New Year meant something. Only in the mountains, where we had come from, would nothing really change.

The following evening, when we arrived back at their apartment in Teramo, Christian and Patricia were out. They had gone to a religious vigil, and left plates of lentils – traditional for that time of year – on the table for us. We ate the lentils with bread, wine and cheese, and watched the big colour television which dominated the kitchen. There was a chat show, compèred by a small bald man surrounded by tall, leggy women in fishnet tights. It featured dances, a gambling wheel and crooners, and was interrupted once for a news report of drownings off Rio de Janeiro, where a ferry had capsized. There were pictures of the corpses, zoomed in on by cameras as they were slung in crates into the back of a mortuary van. Then we were back to the bald compere, the tuxedoed girls. It summed up Italy in a way – the whipped cream of the dolce vita, the razzmatazz of fake passion, and the grim reality coming through in flashes, from below.

'So where did you get to?' Patricia asked when she and Christian came back.

'Bologna.'

'Polonia. Eh, Polonia? How did you get so far?'

We apologized, as we were always doing, for our Italian accents. Christian waved it aside, and treated us to a discourse on the language. Only on television, he said, was there a standard Italian. Everyone still spoke the dialect of their region, all but incomprehensible to each other. Of these, the Tuscan was considered the finest in terms of clarity of accent and depth of meaning. It was the dialect out of which Dante had written the *Commedia*, the first synthesis that could be called modern Italian. But his own favourite poet was Carducci, whose rolling lines he quoted as emblematic of the rolling landscapes, the long avenues of trees, in Carducci's heartland up around Pisa. He was a delightful man, with a saintly gentleness and delicacy of spirit. Unlike most of the people we now knew in the Abruzzo, he had no particular axe to grind.

17

THE NEW YEAR BEGAN in an atmosphere of convalescence. The whole village, besides ourselves, was convalescing from the flu. A winter sun irradiated it, like an outpatients department in which the walking wounded moved around stiffly, rheumatically, soaking up energy from its light. Each afternoon a group of village elders, Gegeto among them, took their dogs out for a walk on the mountain road to Poggio. We watched them from afar, labouring along up there at their own pace, pausing to examine this oak tree or that milestone, habitués glorying in their minuscule, lifelong familiarity with every stone and blade of grass on the slopes.

Though it was bitterly cold in the mountains, the skies stayed calm and bright blue through the whole month of January. In the silence of days, we heard icicles crack and shatter on the ground, the slither of snow off roofs. A glorious false spring set in, with the air in the mountains pristine as a concave lens staring into outer space. Freakish violets bloomed, the branches were tasselled with early catkins. When we felt stronger, we too went out for a walk each afternoon along the mountain road. We laid ourselves out on beds of dry leaves and sunbathed, with a circle of snowy peaks around us. We talked of money and the future, and like the rest of the villagers, we talked about America. In February we were going to America, for three weeks, to earn enough money to keep us here through until the summer. We soaked up the warm light, ignoring the danger of snakes in the dead leafage. But always we watched the sun on its narrow winter arc behind the peaks. We followed its withdrawing light down the hill to the village again, for the temperature in the zones of shadow had already sunk below zero. Dead finches, bright blobs of plumage and heart failure, littered the icy road.

It was the dead of winter in the village. Out behind the church, Silvio whacked desultorily at a few bits of wood. His family had not, after all, had to go down and live in Montorio, on the floor of the valley. A man at the lower end of the village opened an unofficial vegetable shop with supplies he had kept hidden, until now, in his garage. With these, he cheerfully fleeced a captive market, such as ourselves and the old who couldn't get away. In a meadow below the village, the man who siphoned off our water had decided to train one of his horses. He had it running endless circles around a fixed pole in the centre, from which he controlled it by a rope tied to its neck, and a whip whose crack we could hear at regular intervals. Apart from these spasms of activity, however, the village was in suspended animation. Each morning, in the bright silence of forenoon in the empty bar, an old man from the upper village, immaculately dressed, partook, alone, ceremoniously and at leisure, of a glass of white wine, and departed again for his house. That was the kind of month it was – a glass of white wine, in the bright, silent void of pure contemplation.

Only once did the larger world intrude. Far away, under other skies, a bomb had blown apart a passenger airliner, killing over two hundred people. Gradually, it became apparent that one of the victims, a teenage girl, had been from the Abruzzo, and from our village in the Abruzzo. The body, after being flown home to Italy, would be brought up here and buried in the cemetery above the village.

On the day of the burial, Gegeto was out on the square with a crowbar, breaking up the impacted blue ice in front of the church door. As he worked, the cortège approached across the mountains, from the direction of Rome and Prato. The hearse, the family cars and the dignitaries with their police escort drew up in the square, filling it for once with the sounds of worldliness. This was newsworthy political misery, unlike the usual political misery the village embodied. For the wealthy relatives, this was obviously their first and last time in the village. After a brief service, the burial took place on a bright blue afternoon, and the mourners were gone as quickly as they had blown in, leaving a couple of journalists, whom we fed at the house, to gather local colour for their stories. After a while, they too were gone, and the place reverted to its winterbound quiet. For the briefest of moments, we had been part of the mesh of global politics.

It had been a long, long time since history had last intruded. In 1943, after his deposition by the Badoglio government, Mussolini had been rescued by the Germans from the mountains above us, and installed as puppet leader of the Salo state in north Italy, until April 1945, when his executed body hung upside down on a butcher's hook in the piazza in Milan. A warning to tyrants. There had been one already from the villages of the Abruzzo who had met a similar end to Mussolini – the bombastic, fantastical Cola Di Renzo in the fourteenth century, also inflamed with the dream of unifying Italy under a reconstituted historical greatness, also a man who confused the Italians with the Romans and paid with his life for the error. It seemed to underlie the mistake of moving beyond the village in the first place. That, at least, is how the villagers saw it.

There had been fighting in the mountains, Cesare told us, during the German occupation. But the Germans had only briefly occupied territories this far south. In the autumn of 1943 L'Aquila had been liberated and the front had moved north. Once, the Germans had come up to Poggio and taken a couple of prisoners, but released them the next day. There had been a resistance movement, he said, but one had to be careful when talking of the resistance. People around here, he said, had joined it for all kinds of reasons, not particularly idealistic ones, more usually for profiteering or the chance to live and work outside the law. He spoke of that time, as the priest did, with something like distaste, as of something shameful, embarrassing, and far in the past.

It was during this empty, quiet time that we got to know Luciano, one of the last living representatives of that past in the village. The front of his house was a suntrap where he took the winter sun in the afternoon with a bottle of wine and his little dog for company. We struck up a conversation in passing one day. He asked us to join him, plied us with wine, and started telling us his life story. As with many people who do not normally talk, once he began it was impossible to stop him.

He had fought, if that is the word, in the last war, one of the millions bled from the villages by Mussolini's call to arms. When he left he was nineteen, when he returned he was thirty. With his cheap shirt and cardboard shoes he had been captured in the Libyan desert. One of the luckier ones, he said, not sent to die in front of Stalingrad. The English had transported him by prison ship to Britain, where, until 1946, he had cooled his heels in a detention camp, doing basic war work and flirting with the English girls who threw in chocolate from the other side of the barbed wire. He had good memories of England and had learned a little of the language – which, naturally, he tried out on us. After his release, he had wandered through the ruins of northern Europe for some years, where young hands like his were in short supply, and became a coalminer in Belgium – he still drew state benefits from his Belgian work. Eventually, like thousands of other displaced Italians, he drifted back to his country, his home village, unthanked for the sacrifice of the best ten years of his life, married and raised a family here.

Last year his wife had died, and now he was alone. He described the first symptoms of her cancer, and the dark inevitability of her death. There were five children, all grown up and living elsewhere in Italy, who visited him once in a while. It was clear that whatever his war experience meant to him, it was nothing compared to the intensity of his family life. His real loyalty, as with so many Italians we had met, was to the privately human rather than the abstractly political.

When the bottle of wine was finished, he took us indoors for another one. The interior of his house was dark and frugal – a table covered with oilcloth, on which stood a few basic necessities. He was a man alone, waiting for death. His windows to the outside world were closed. He took us down to his cellar under the house, a dry place with an odour of stone and old wood. It was full of things laid aside from his working life – a big stone quern, leather harness, earthenware jugs. From one of the jugs he poured some white wine fermented from the grapes off his little trellis of vines in front of the house. As he handed us the bottle, sealed with a clasp, he offered us a drink for the road.

'We went to war,' he said suddenly, 'with empty bellies, and Mussolini's visons in our heads. But would we have seen the visions if our bellies hadn't been empty? If you want to know, that's what the war was to us – wine on a empty stomach.'

On the night of the feast of San Antonio in the middle of January, we heard the distant clatter of drumsticks, and the sound of off-key singing moving here and there about the village. Later, when all seemed to have gone quiet, we heard a thump on the front door. When we opened it, half the village burst into the San Antonio song, while Nello flailed away on a tin drum. Ours was the last house in the village, and they had had a drink in every one. They were fit to be tied.

We invited them in for a night-cap. They were all more or less of the same generation – the women who ran the *co-operativa*, Nello, whom we had seen rolling in the snow outside the bar that afternoon, Laura and Pino, the newly-weds from last autumn, Silvio, in a state of benevolent drunkenness, others we knew who worked on the mountain tunnel, and finally Cesare, looking out of place among the hard men of the village. They drank off their glasses at a gulp, and launched into a final rendition of the song.

'If it was Padre Simone,' Nello said, 'he would have kept us outside and listened to us through the window.'

They were interested in everything – our books, the decorations on the walls, the furniture and ecclesiastical bric-à-brac. Through their eyes, we saw again what a strange house it was, and how it must once have been held in awe, of which even now some traces remained.

'You may not believe it,' one of the women said, 'but for many of us, this is the first time we have ever been inside this house.'

Laura and Pino invited everyone back to their house for pasta. It was a freezing night of inky blackness, crusted with stars. Ahead of us, two women supported Silvio up the icy road to the top end of the village. Although Silvio was the wild man, it was clear he was much loved. His extremity of behaviour brought out protectiveness towards him, especially in women. He apologized for the episode of the wood and said, with great dignity, that it had been his fault. Then a spasm came over him and he clutched the side of his face.

'It's my teeth,' he gasped. 'I suffer terribly from decay in my teeth. I'm a sick man, you know . . .'

Since their wedding, Laura and Pino had worked on their house. It was tiny, a one up and one down with a kitchen and bathroom. Outcrops of wild Abruzzo rock jutted into the rooms and were incorporated into the design. It was like being inside a submarine, but a cosy submarine negotiating its way through the freezing waters of the Abruzzo night. The men squashed in around the little table, cracking ribald jokes about the Pope while the women served wine and spaghetti, and hunks of crude sausage from the pig Giambattista had killed.

Cesare, through these hearty proceedings, looked lost and alone. Though he represented the village in the Poggio commune, he was not one of the boys. His mental sophistication set him apart, and he could manage only a smile of wry embarrassment as the others crudely lambasted religion, the state and central government. Their jokes were unfunny, they went on too long, and there was always one particularly slow local man – the '*bombardiere*' they called him, in an ironical attempt to make him seem clever and conspiratorial – who hadn't understood the first time and needed it all spelt out again. The '*bombardiere*' had a hook in place of his left hand, which had been blown off by an explosive he had mishandled. After a while Cesare slipped off, without being missed.

In a way, the village was the least private place we could have chosen to hide away and write in. Our typewriters blasted out daily over the wintry silence of the piazza, and the villagers outside wondered, no doubt, if some kind of hex was being put on them. Once again that night we were asked, but casually, what it was we were writing, and our answers got lost in the general uproar. Unlike Cesare, we were only here for a year. And for the time being at least, we had been taken to heart.

18

THE TREES ON THE MOUNTAIN road to Poggio were dwarf oak. Forests of them extended up the slopes. Even now, in late winter, with the configurations of the landscape hard and bare, they had kept enough of their burnished golden leafage to shade us when the sun was at its height, and the ground beneath them was a vast natural mattress of dry windfalls from the autumn before. The trunks of the little trees were tough, gnarled and silvery. They insinuated themselves through crevices in the disintegrating rock as the taproots forced their way down to whatever nourishment there was in the thin layer of soil. This wild network of roots between outcrops of pink and yellow rock held the slopes together and prevented them from slithering away en masse. As we lay out there, we heard tiny rustlings of disintegration and consolidation around us.

Besides the big realities of the mountains, there was the microscopic realm. A particular bright green lizard lived under a flat stone at a certain place along the road. Once found, it was always there. There were the places where water issued from the ground, and there were the routes snakes took. The same few trout hung motionless in the bridge pool, summer, autumn and winter. In the house, there were flying beetles. We had seen them bright green against the glass of the windows in the autumn, with winter building up in the mountain skies beyond, and waited for

144

them to turn white and die. Kept alive by the heat of the stove, they buzzed companionably around the living room at night. Colonies of ants swarmed under the kitchen door and traced faint lines of coming and going to and from the blackened stone hearth. With these little things inside and out, and the squirrel running about in the attic, we cultivated an intimacy of sorts, sometimes irritated but always real, so that their own patterns of life interwove with ours. They were the thin end of the very physical wedge the mountains drove into us over the months.

The mountains were locked in snow, but the fine dry weather had already melted a little of it. The torrent through the bridge was swollen with a greenish effervescent snowmelt that oxygenated the pools and made a steady, distant roar in the calm blackness of the frozen nights. It was an early sign of spring, and it would continue through to May, when the peaks turned green again. Runoff opened new channels through the forests, which were filled with the primal sound of water. The carcass of a sheep, the skeleton of a car or a fridge, flung into the ravines, lent a biblical, escatological overtone of flood and chaos to the natural wildness of the waterfalls.

On Sundays, we hitched a lift with whoever was driving up to Poggio, and walked back down the five winding kilometres of mountain road, with the rumpled chain of the Apennines, a dazzle of snow, always to our north. The road itself had only been built after the Second World War. Before it there had been a cart-track up from Montorio – a day's journey then, half an hour's vertiginous drive now. Old milestones, half buried in moss and earth, still showed the older route. As we descended, we could see the lines of abandoned roads and sheeptracks like a loose webbing through the forest, converging here and there on the ruins of a mountain shelter. Sometimes, we rested in those shelters, with their bundles of faggots and their heaped fodder against walls of cut stone and occasionally the rusted remnants of a stove. They were empty as the chapels in the mountains were empty. The life of religious worship, like the life of pasturage, had left traces of its desolated infrastructure everywhere.

Much had passed away up here, or refined itself into attitudes, morose silences. Poggio was famously morose, guarding its essence of brigandage and freedom from whoever were the powers that be at any given time. Its withdrawal, so to speak, from historical space and time, was a legend. Pigeons roosted in the gutted upstairs rooms of abandoned houses. Cats intrigued in the cellars. Half the village had boarded up its front doors and gone to America through sheer necessity, only to return as and when it could, always preserving the crossply of intermarriage, even out there in the great spaces of America. The people here had known suffering, but the breath of aristocracy had blown on them too in earlier centuries. Their suffering hadn't broken their pride in themselves, as to some extent it had in our own village. Instead, it had transfigured them into poets and philosophers.

One of these was Renato.

Renato was the carpenter of Poggio. Because his house was adjacent to the church, he had the office of handyman there too, a post not without responsibilities given the earthquake damage that ran like cracks through its structure. On the day in February we visited Renato, shortly before going to America, the church still had its crib at the back, which he had made out of sacking. Padre Giuseppe, who had first taken us to Poggio the previous summer, lived in the remnants of a ducal tower on the other side of the church, feeding an enormous number of local cats who had joined him there in his retirement. All this area Renato had more or less assumed responsibility for, although it wasn't how he earned his living. Like the other able bodied of Poggio, he supported his family by working on the tunnel.

At the entrance to the plot of land on which his house was built, he had installed a wooden gate in Wild West style, with a big wagon wheel in the middle – a reminder of his years in America. There were outhouses, a-swarm with half-wild cats, and a rough wooden table he had built for outdoor eating. The house itself was a warren of tiny thick-walled rooms warmed by an almost permanent fire in the chimney-breast downstairs. As usual, three generations lived in this house – his only child Lucio, aged nineteen, Renato himself and his wife Lia, and her mother Silvia, a woman of eighty who performed the office of keeper of the fire.

Silvia, a dialect poet, was a woman of fame in the locality. I had heard her composing verses 'al fresco' at the dinner table and laughing, toothlessly and uproariously, at the results. The dialect itself was a mix of Latin, French and German influences left by the various conquerors who had been this way over the centuries. About all I could distinguish were the rhymes. She was said to have written beautiful poems of local inspiration and her presence was of extraordinary intensity. Her eyes were bright and her skin, when I kissed her in greeting was soft and youthful as a child's. She had been through the experience of emigration and factory work in American cities, she had married and raised a family. At eighty, her sense of the passing hour was terribly acute. Often, when we said goodbye to her, she cried, not out of sentimentality but from genuine emotion, the fear of never seeing us again, the fear of death. She had achieved the impossible, a rare completeness of humanity.

Renato's life, on the other hand, was a broken arc, and the cause of the rupture lay across the ocean in Canada. He had gone there on the migratory wave of the Fifties. He had been through the night shifts as a casual labourer. With his brother, he had established a small construction company which had prospered. One summer, when he had come back to Poggio with his family, his brother had legally done him out of his share in the company, and left him broke. He had no option but to start again as a carpenter in Poggio. This had happened ten years ago, and he was still swallowing his bitterness. He had never been back to Canada again but he and his wife hoped to raise the money in time for their twenty-fifth wedding anniversary.

In spite of himself, he had come to appreciate the beauty and coherence of his life in Poggio. His balcony, his plot of land overlooking the mountains to the north, had made a wiser man of him. He liked to generalize, not unkindly, about life, particularly at the end of a long meal – and the meals we ate with him in the mountains always trailed away in long, meditative codas, with grace-notes in the form of fruits, grappa or a mountain liqueur distilled from one of the berries of the high valley. Life was good on the whole, he had come to conclude. Here he had a community, his child had been reared with a sense of the place to which he belonged, and without the disorienting pressures of an accelerated lifestyle. Renato could be irritable – against his son, for instance – but he had lost his deep anger against life. He had found, in the mountains, detachment and peace.

We ate at the outdoor table, overlooking the mountains, under a still-weak February sun, with a breeze riffling the white tablecloth. Chimney smoke drifted lazily over the roofs of the inhabited houses. Now and again the breeze brought us the ghost of a sound, the noise of snow-water in the valley. Up the town, an old bell clanked out an irrelevant hour. And the dishes came and went, the glasses were refilled, the daydream that was life gave itself air and space.

'Ya wanna *birra?*' Renato asked occasionally, in the hybrid English and Italian he had retained from his Toronto years. 'Ya wanna *bicciera d'aqua?*'

Upstairs, through an open window, his son strummed an electric guitar. The songs were fifteen years out of date, but that was true of Italy as a whole, not just the Abruzzo. With these songs as the basis of a repertoire, Lucio, in his father's car, took a skiffle band on tour through various watering-holes in the mountains at weekends, when he was home from his engineering studies at L'Aquila university. He was part of the agnostic generation, but there seemed to be no tension between himself and his churchgoing parents in the matter of religion. While they were at Mass, he was up the town with his friends at the bar, having a coffee. In terms of observance, the family meal was a more sacred occasion than the rites celebrated in the church.

After the meal, we went with Renato to the house of a man who specialized in making spirits from the herbs and berries that bloomed behind Poggio, in various hidden places known only to himself. His liqueurs – he made only a few bottles a year – were much in demand. By good luck, I had come into possession of one myself the previous autumn, a fiery distillate of juniper, the colour of icewater, in a plain glass bottle. I had eked it out, nip by nightly nip, over the best part of a month.

This man lived on the other side of Poggio, facing the peaks to the south. We passed through lightless medieval alleys crusted with snow, and knocked at a low door in a wall of tiny entrances. This one had '1492', the date of original construction, on the stone lintel. When the door opened, and we stepped inside from the dark street, we were met by a blaze of light from the big windows facing the mountains, a sense of space and levitation. The house was built into the rockface and the rooms were connected vertically, by spiral staircases through the floors. He too was a carpenter who had come home from America and had reared his family. The interior of the house was his work of art, and he lived in it with the silver-haired eminence so many Italian men assume in later age. There was a sense of wholeness and peace, reinforced by the poetry of the liqueur he poured for us, clear in its little glasses on the table.

'We only had to leave here once,' his wife said. 'When the earthquakes came that killed so many in Avezzano and Naples. We had to stay away for a week, but the structure was intact.'

Outside, through the blinding white of the snow up-valley, we could see the lines where the mountain had been twisted by the force of earth movements. It was the sword of Damocles that hung over the Abruzzo villages, and it fell with the irregularity of fate. Now there was peace, however, and the plots of land in the high valley beyond the house were being readied for spring – little black rectangles of earth, patches of vines, vegetable plots. It was still too early in the year for us to go hiking higher, in the valley behind Poggio. But for now it was enough to see it through the plateglass window – the special intensity Poggio distilled up there in its own light, like a mica grain in the mountains. When they weren't being struck by blows of fate, the ordinary, like Renato and his friend, who had built their philosophical shelves out into the absolute, were the envy of millionaires.

19

IN LATE FEBRUARY, WE LEFT for America. As soon as we reached it, we mailed a flurry of postcards to the people we knew in the villages. They had asked us to do this as a reminder of their own time in America, or their dream of going to America, or the relatives they still had in America who would return to the village in the summer. This summer it would be a different group. It took those who lived and worked in America at least two years to save for the trip. As we mailed the cards in the big, anonymous American post offices, we felt we were inhabiting, not a new space, but an extension of the psychic space of the village. America imbued the conversations we heard in the village with yearning, disillusionment and loss. It was supposed to make the difference between success and failure in life. For the three weeks of our visit, instead of living in the village itself, we inhabited its fourth dimension.

We entered it through the needle's eye of Customs and Immigration at Kennedy Airport, and almost immediately found ourselves on a night internal flight to Washington DC, with the lights of Manhattan and Jersey drifting astern, and the lights of smaller towns spreading like connective tissue through the dark landmass below us. As we came down into Washington, these generalized lights gave way to hundreds of particularized, speeding lights on the highways, converging, dispersing, criss-crossing and overpassing, like

152

atomic particles let loose in a giant cyclotron. American space was that cyclotron, and we, like the others processed through Kennedy, had been let loose to zoom around inside it for a while. Unlike the space of the village, American space was speed, movement, dispersal.

It was still winter in Washington. A polar wind blew off the Potomac, up the length of Arlington to the Dupont Circle. More than a wind, it was an icy transcontinental blast that made nothing of the scurrying, winterclad humans on those streets of offices and ministries that closed at six, when the city reverted to primordial desertion. Streetwalkers, tough as nails in tight miniskirts, braved the weather for the passing trade in congressional aides – need consorting with power. Here, it was either success or failure. There was no middle ground.

Snowstorms kept us grounded an extra day, before we flew through to North Carolina. There, while we earned what was to keep us in the village for a few more months, the snow and ice melted, vivid birds appeared on the greening trees, and the southern spring began. Schools opened, and roads were unblocked. Downtown Raleigh had experienced a tornado a few months before, and the litter of destruction was still evident. Even if it hadn't been, our impression would have been the same – of a stageset with nothing behind it but unpopulated emptiness. Solidity, permanence, the continued existence of man-made surroundings as we knew them in the Abruzzo, meant nothing here. Raleigh, the capital of North Carolina, seemed like a town constructed yesterday, which tomorrow might be gone.

In this space, full of transience and movement, we passed

two weeks. Where we lived, the houses were spaced acres apart. No one seemed to know who lived on either side of him. Huge cars glided in and out of driveways, and disappeared into remote-controlled garages, with a week's supply of food from the supermarket. Apart from work and shopping, it seemed the rest of outside existence was filtered into these houses through thirty-six channels of colour television. They had been planted in the middle of a wilderness with which they had no real connection. Nothing could have been further from the litigious closeness of our Abruzzo village, soldered by love and suffering to its patches of backyard soil.

Our work over, we headed north again. In Washington a thaw had blown the trees into tentative blossom, with the ice still on the pavements. But in New York it was winter. The trees of Central Park were iron-grey, the pavements of Fifth Avenue shone with a mica sparkle of rime. Speed, noise, dimension – New York was a bigger stageset, but still a stageset. Through it blew the same transcontinental breezes, icy and inhuman.

At night, we slept in the air-conditioned warmth of a hotel room. Our bodies generated static, from the artificial fibres of carpets and bedclothes. In the mornings, we breakfasted across the street. After three weeks, we were still living at the slowed metabolic rate of the Abruzzo. While we ate our bacon and eggs, our hash browns and maple syrup, and drank our bottomless cups of coffee, two, sometimes three different New Yorkers had replaced each other in the adjacent booths. Here, one ate to work. We thought of our meals with Renato, at his outdoor table in the mountains, and read again on the wall of the diner instructions for helping those who choked on their food.

We had never left the village – we had simply visited its fourth dimension. America was that fourth dimension, just as it was for thousands of other villages in Indochina, Puerto Rico, the west of Ireland. In that fourth dimension strange effects occurred – the gap between material desire and its immediate satisfaction closed, but the gap between the heart and its origins expanded. The space of that fourth dimension was vast and lonely, a physical not a psychic space. Physically, life expanded here, psychically, it shrank. Only when you returned to your place of origin did you recover your human scale again, as the fourth dimension reverted to a half-forgotten buzz in your ears.

In late March, with that buzzing still in our ears, we flew back into Rome. Spring had arrived ahead of us, softly greening the countryside on the way in from the airport, tasselling the trees on the Via Condotti and in the Borghese Gardens. After the insane geometry of New York, Rome, the mother of cities, was blossom, fragrance, Mediterranean femininity. After the roar of the traffic on Riverside Drive, the buzzing of scooters on Via Flaminia, the beepings of little *cinquecentos*, seemed like a return to normality.

Soft morning light, the subliminal cheeping of sparrows, lay across the streets and piazzas. Easter confections, whorled in giftwrapping, were on display in the shop windows. The tables had been moved on to the pavements. Men sat at them and chatted, as if the street, with its patches of sun through greenery, really belonged to them rather than they to the street. The tables were spread with heavy white linen. Beside them, napkins folded over one arm, waiters stood like priests before the altar of a sacred rite. When we were ready to eat we sat down, at some ordinary place. Heavy cutlery was put before us, bread and wine, glasses. We felt again the reality, the sacredness of food and drink. Time itself, and the leisure to contemplate it, were restored to us. Italy was measure, after the unbridled energies of the fourth dimension.

The following afternoon, we took a bus east through the Apennines to the Adriatic side. A thrilling ride, a return from inflation to proportion, from human distortion in a magnified space, to life, albeit harsh, on a normal scale. Did the many who had come back this way to the village feel as I felt that day? The onset of spring in the mountains was still retarded. The higher we went, the more barren it was, with snow on the peaks and a few stunted trees in the rocky scree of the passes. We emerged from the tunnel to a shock of early blossom and green on the Adriatic side. Near Montorio, the apple orchards were foaming white. Spring was advancing into the mountains, but gradually. With every stage closer to the village we felt a deepening of physical contact with the landscape, and a diminution of the vacuum we had come from.

The next day was Palm Sunday. Stefania had arranged sprigs of local plants around the coping of the old well in the square. At eleven, under a pale spring sun, we stood in a loose circle as the priest in white robes blessed them with holy water. Those who wanted them came forward then, and took sprigs for the walls of their homes. All the local plants were there, with the sap of early spring oozing from them – fuzzy golden willows, and the grey branches of olives that stood outside the cycle of seasons altogether.

Snow and ice had melted off the cobbles of the square. Here, the passage of time was still marked by ritual observance. Even those not attending that little ceremony were marked by it, and knew it was going on. In a way, they depended on it. It gave structure to their lives, even if it was a liturgical structure they professed to have abandoned. There had been other ceremonies earlier in the year – Candlemas, when Gegeto rooted in the junk under our stairs to find a few candles worth blessing in the dark, freezing church, or the Blessing of the Animals, which happened while we were away in America. We had come back from that other extension of the village into the future, to this one, which extended into the past.

That afternoon, we went for a walk as far as the bridge. Above us, the peaks were still snowy, but in the dwarf forests around us it had melted and given way to thick new grass and yellow sunbursts of primroses in the clefts between rocks. The brief season of the violets had come and gone, but something more delicate was already taking its place – wild cyclamens in groups, the colours of fine liqueurs, suspended on their fragile stems. These early arrivals were the advance guard of an amazing botanical uprush that the dry soil of the Abruzzo was to foster in the coming months.

The house, when we came back to it, smelt of warm absence, a compound of dust, kerosene fumes and dried vegetables. Its sandstone walls, in their rough-hewn crudeness, were more beautiful to us than all the architecture we had seen on our travels. They had solidity, a kind of permanence. They were something to lean on. A green shadow traced itself on the far wall of the kitchen – Gegeto's fig tree, coming into leaf outside the window. On the stone floor, an army of ants traced a line from the hearth to the worm-eaten gap at the base of the back door, through which fresh green grass was peeping. Upstairs, there was a new silence – our friend the squirrel, who had irritated and entertained us since autumn, had abandoned his winter quarters.

In the evening after we had cooked and eaten a simple meal in the kitchen, Gegeto tapped on the window and handed us the post that had accumulated while we were away. As we were reading it, Olympia and her husband Carlo arrived with a bag of fresh vegetables from the kitchen garden they cultivated just below the village. They had come up for the first time since last autumn, to air their house for their return in a few weeks, to check their hens and beehives, to do repairs after the winter. They were on their way back down to Teramo now, and they had just called in to see if we were still alive after the rigours of the Abruzzo winter, if the cloth over the fireplace had worked, if the stove had kept us warm. Yes, we were indeed. We had just returned from the fourth dimension and we were still alive. In fact, we had never been more alive.

20 EASTER CAME EARLY, AT the beginning of April. From the stripped altar on Holy Thursday to the lush floral extravaganza it became the following Sunday, two days intervened. During those days, the church smelled of fresh clay Gegeto had provided from his garden. Without reference to her benefactor, Stefania worked the cut yellow blooms and green sprigs into patterns around the altar, while the shrouded statues loomed in the background. Earth and spirit conspired, if a bit unwillingly.

Around this time, the first visitors of the year showed up. We looked across the road and saw a wealthy Roman with a gold chain around his neck whom we had last seen the previous summer, when he threw his villa open to the local people for all-night parties. He was sunning himself on the veranda outside the bar, and reading his personal copy of the Roman *Messagero*. The rest of the village contented itself with the week-old back issues left in the bar by whoever happened to have thrown them aside there – in this way we had learnt, several days afterwards, of a number of major world events. But our Roman was back among us again, with his big car, his Armani shirt and his deep voice shouting for coffee to be brought out to him on the veranda. He alone took the reading of newspapers seriously, and regarded it as a daily, almost sacred rite.

If Caesar was among us, he hadn't much competition from

our local version of Christ. This consisted of a reclining
figure housed for most of the year in a glass recess in one
wall of the church. Blood, luridly red, seeped from his many
wounds, and his face expressed irritation, perhaps at being
cooped up in so uncongenial a tomb. In this irritation at the
order of things he was joined by the devils, and, as I had
noticed from their daily expressions, by the villagers themselves. Theirs was a Christ of the minor irritations upon
which, daily, they were crucified. In any case, he was about
to be given his annual airing, and for this purpose Gegeto
had placed a wooden pallet in front of the recess. On this
pallet, carried shoulder high about our irritable village, he
would embody the Resurrection.

On the evening of Holy Saturday, by the old well in the
piazza, Gegeto lit a bundle of faggots – the paschal fire. Its
yellow flames wavered in the warm grey air, and those
standing around fanned it with pieces of old newspapers and
the expert technique acquired at their own chimneybreasts.
The priest blessed the fire itself and the Easter water the
villagers had brought in stoppered bottles and containers.
From the fire. Gegeto lit the large paschal candle. From this
large candle, the villagers lit their smaller ones, and the
procession of lit candles entered the church, where Mass was
said. It was after this Mass that the wooden Christ was
carried out into the evening air and off on its circuit of the
village.

For once, on Easter Sunday, everything went well. There
was a large congregation, and the sermon floated over it
without tremors of discord. There was even some singing –
not by the villagers, but by a few lady visitors whose
powerful voices soared without embarrassment to the very

highest registers. Many of the congregation had with them Easter cakes to be blessed. Afterwards, over black coffee and biscuits, a large crowd gathered in the kitchen to pay their respects. Before leaving the village, the priest made a point of crossing to the bar and sharing a joke with the Roman businessman.

Of the drunken, cheerful mob who had burst through our door that far-off night in January, however, who had looked with amazement at the inner strangeness of the house, not one had been part of the crowd in the kitchen. Only that afternoon, when the priest was gone and the village was quiet, did we hear a knock on the door. It was Luciano, the last of Mussolini's soldiers, delightedly drunk since his son had come to visit him that morning, and bearing as a gift to us, Easter wine and cake.

The bar had come back to life. It was our Via Veneto, our Boulevard Saint Germain. The philosophers of the village gathered there, to fulminate against existence. Winter had shrunk it to a yellow light or two over a couple of card games, but it had found its second wind. Adolescents on motorbikes hung around outside it, and took the local girls for quick spins. Others breezed in from neighbouring villages to check the place out. It had a whiff of sex and wildness, of loudmouthed defiance, of kicking against the pricks. It was the point at which everyday life, usually after a string of whiskies, became spirit.

It was gearing itself up for a crucial season. The coming summer would be its proving ground, when it would be watched by its jealous rivals, the family in the square. It had won the licence for the public telephone, and it was making plans, in secret, for a completely new look on the outside. The committee of young women who ran it had decided among themselves that rather than get entangled with the local bureaucracy for planning permission, they would present it as a *fait accompli*. So, one mild spring night, when the police and administrators of Poggio were safely in their beds, a team of workmen aided by lamps set about the walls and roof, sandblasting and spraypainting for all they were worth, until by the first light the following day, the bar presented itself to the world as a salmon pink apparition, a beacon through mountain space for miles around.

This was only the beginning. A lorry drove up one afternoon and began unloading the jukebox and the assortment of one-armed bandits that had been taken away in September. It wasn't long before these were being tried out – especially the jukebox, with its assortment of ancient hits – but only for an hour or two in the afternoons, before the children had been called in for their evening meal. As long as school lasted, the village stayed peaceful during the day. Only in June, a month before the actual ending of term, did the village declare unofficial holidays for its children, and *bel canto* wafted from the jukebox through the village at all hours. By July and August, when the crowds were home from America and the crescendo came, we would be long gone.

Whatever people wanted in the way of entertainment, the bar was going to give it. Workmen were employed to construct a small wooden alley for bowls, with a couple of lights strung over the surrounding wire mesh. Late into the night, the older men played there in a pool of insectivorous light. The thud of bowls against the plank at the end of the alley lulled us to sleep through the spring nights, with the double note of a cuckoo up in the woods.

It was warm enough now to sit out at night in front of the bar. But most of its business was still indoors and by day. There was hardly a single person in the village, young or old, who didn't at one time or another fancy an ice-cream. To its chocolate, strawberry, lemon and vanilla flavours, the bar had added apricot, *frutti di bosco*, pistachio and half a dozen others. It was sold with the same sense of importance as wine or whisky. Grown men, the hardened cases of the village, were not above joining grannies and toddlers in a lemon and strawberry cone. Possession of this universal symbol of Italian innocence caught them, momentarily, with their trousers down. It brought out the child in everyone.

One night in April, the first dance in the village for many years was held, on an unweeded concrete space at the back of the bar. Once, when the bar had been a school, there had been a ball court there, and a couple of unsmashed overhead lights illuminated the waltzes, tangos and foxtrots as the villagers, with closed faces, moved each other about. The bar had provided demijohns of cheap wine and glasses, and connected a loudspeaker for the music to an outside wall. It had the sedate air of a try-out for louder, future dances for which a licence had not yet been granted, and it folded, shyly and gracefully, just before midnight. There was a pathos about it, as of a dance in an institution for the clinically depressed, whose self-image has been damaged and who are slowly and tentatively coming back to life. If the women of the *co-operativa* had done nothing else but this, they had done a great deal. Something good had returned to the village.

Through April, the mountains changed. An invisible hand turned the temperature up, not spectacularly, but significantly. As in a greenhouse, everything reacted. The nights were still cool enough for the stove to need lighting, but there was a new warmth in the days. The village women were outdoors, working the black clay of kitchen gardens at the backs of houses, their skirts hitched up around their waists, their monumental white legs astraddle the drills. The worked plots were miracles of efficient horticulture on a tiny scale – patches of potatoes, purple cabbages and lettuce, neatly tied vines. Underground, but visible as a slight earth tremor, moles tunnelled through the clay. Everything was on the move, in that brief, vivid season.

Apparational against the black earth, fruit trees blossomed white and pink, a moment of fantastic delicacy with the tough jagged mountains in the background. A fine green fuzz of spring invested the willow trees in the paddocks where the horses were being exercised. Cats sunned themselves. Dogs panted along paths that in a month would be overgrown. It was the moment of softening in the Abruzzo, after the bareness of winter. The buds in the oak forests were at bursting point – a single night of rain would bring them all out together, in a shock of green. There would be shade for the horses and dogs, in the white haze of May heat.

Work resumed on the tunnel. The roads up there were a muddy yellow clabber, and what was left of the snow had solidified into white frozen blocks of abstract sculpture. Outside our house, the drone of heavy lorries had resumed, sending deep vibrations through the walls and rattling the windows. The village, after its fashion, had gone back to work. A few lorryloads of soaked green wood were already being brought down, to be stacked and dried for the autumn.

The Sicilian orange merchant disappeared, and the travelling shop, with its blast of absurd music, rolled into the square again. The bald shopkeeper was still there, large as life, but his whippet-like wife had been replaced by a daughter, also famished-looking, who filled the local women in on how her mother's seventh pregnancy had gone.

All this time, we still lived in deep silence. Only the arrival of the birds from Africa broke it. Suddenly they were everywhere, whizzing and chittering in the space between houses, zooming up to their clay nests under the eaves – darker swifts in the distance, and nearer, the creamy-breasted swallows. They fed off clouds of insects above the tops of trees that fell away into the ravine. They were there in their hundreds, and their subliminal electricity put an end, once and for all, to the wintry silence of the village.

Our house was an ideal nesting site for these birds. The sandstone blocks of its walls were loosely fitted together, with deep crevices in between. The roof, in a state of collapse, and the shattered chimney outworks, could have sheltered whole colonies of them. As a house, we were old, warm and congenial, and the silence of our recent desertion by the squirrel was soon replaced by the light, sipping sounds of swifts coming and going. Smashed eggshells, the missed chances of spring, lay in their own glaur on the ground outside.

In the vast, blue quiet of dawn in the mountains, we had a visitation, repeating itself, at the same hour, for two or three weeks. An invisible battering at a windowpane somewhere about the house, fading away after half an hour or so. It soon became clear that a bird was flying blindly against the pane of one window, again and again, until it injured itself and flew away. Perhaps, when a pane was broken, it had nested in the house the previous spring, and it had come back by instinct to the same place. Its arrival out of the blue unsettled us, and we cast about in the back of our minds for superstitions. Was it good luck or bad? Other spirits than ours were interested in this house. We would not be here forever.

21 WE HEARD THE POUNDING on the door. Anyone who visited had to pound on the door, unless we were in the kitchen, when they could tap on the window. But in the mornings, though we thought of ourselves as early risers, the village regarded as, not unkindly, as lieabeds. Our wooden front door had to be pummelled good and hard to make any impression on us at that hour. This morning the pummelling was followed by the voice of Alessandra, and my wife went down in her nightdress to let her in. As I dressed I could hear them talking in the kitchen, and the sound of Alessandra's histrionics, punctuated by fits of crying.

'She has cancer of the breast,' Deirdre told me. 'They will have to remove it.' Alessandra sat hunched over a cup of tea at the table, saying nothing. For the moment, she let my wife do the talking for her. It seemed there had been a lump there, or the suspicion of a lump, for the past couple of years, but Alessandra had concealed the fact from herself, from others and from the medical profession, in the hope that it would go away by itself. The concealment and the hidden fears had been, at least partly, the root of her wild swings of mood. Needless to say, the lump had not gone away. By the time she had taken it to the doctor, surgical removal of the breast had become necessary. The diagnosis had only come through that morning. Ours were by no means the first shoulders she had cried on.

She met this blow with the defencelessness of a child, collapsing into tears and loud, shameless lamentation. There was something almost noble about it, for if death were involved, then reason was useless and all that was left was a scream. So she panicked like a child, just as she had once stroked our hair and clothes in curiosity like a child, or poked my wife in the stomach, or fought with her own children over a pair of boots. She had a child's phobia about hospitals too. Since her father had died there, she couldn't bring herself to enter one, not even to visit her own mother when she went in for tests. Only recently, Stefania, her best friend in the village, suffering from a mountain sickness involving tinnitus of the ears and imbalance, had spent eleven days untreated and undiagnosed in the ward of a public hospital in Teramo, before discharging herself in despair. Into this world Alessandra was headed, like a child in a dark wood.

Bad as these things were, they were details beside her central preoccupation – the loss of her feminine identity, the physical womanhood on which, for her, that identity was based. Besides the loss of a breast, there would be the effects of the chemotherapy to which she would be subjected, by injection, once every two weeks. She would lose all her hair, they had told her. Her skin would turn yellow like parchment, her bowels would clam up. And her husband, she asked, how could he go on living with a disfigured wreck of a woman? No, he was too handsome a man. He would certainly leave her for one of the younger women of the village.

'How would *YOU* feel,' she demanded, pointing between my legs, 'if *THAT* was taken away from you?'

After this outburst she went away sadly, and we didn't see her for a couple of days. Then she reappeared in the Land Rover driven by her husband. She was going on leave – infinite leave, as she put it without humour – and she had come to hand over to her successor, an unshaven, slightly imbecilic man with sly, porcine eyes set in an overfed face, a born occupier of minor bureaucratic posts who, unlike Alessandra, settled happily into the inertia demanded by the position. Although we didn't like him, we had to admit he did the job more efficiently than she did. But without her the village wasn't the same. We were never again to hear her shouts outside the house in the morning, or wonder, in the greyness of winter, if she was wearing yellow or black.

A couple of days later, at her husband Stefano's request, we went over to eat with the family in Prato. The atmosphere was funereal. Alessandra speechlessly pushed a mop around the floor, as if the habits of a lifetime could ward off the ordeal she was facing. By sheer force of habit she prepared a meal and set it before ourselves and her unnaturally quiet children, while Stefano tried desperately to lighten the atmosphere. Even the old woman in black, sensing for once that someone beside herself might die, made an effort to be gay. All in all, it was an unhappy occasion.

Then she was gone. Occasionally people in the village asked after her, but as a presence she had vanished. Once or twice, Stefania drove over to Prato to find out what was happening, or we telephoned from the house. But the news was equivocal, non-committal. She was in a private clinic in Rome, Stefano was sleeping in the room there, the old woman was looking after the children. In the tiny community of the village, it was as if she was already dead.

Besides Alessandra, there were other village women whose lives we followed with the same interest as they followed ours. Not so much the old women, the keepers of the fire, but those in the thick of marriage and child-rearing, for whom the future still seemed, however improbably, a field of choice. They could still go mad, murder or be murdered by their husbands, or simply run away, with or without their children. In the mornings, they pushed their infants up and down the green stretch of road beyond the village, or stood around the travelling shop buying groceries. They fell, roughly speaking, into two categories.

The first and most obvious were the iron women. They appeared to have accepted their role as childbearers, meal providers and emotional, occasionally even physical punchbags for their husbands as their designated lot in life. Their hair was cropped, their expressions not unkind but hardened, neutralized, and their bodies tanklike. They were human shock absorbers, sprung for heavy-duty motherhood, quietly contemptuous of their moody, jobless husbands, and ready at any moment to take over the reins. Among them were Silvio's wife, and her cousin, a woman with a brow like a battering ram who reared her children in the same household. There was also, more remarkably perhaps, the wife of the 'bombardiere'.

She astonished us by addressing us one day in perfect English with an American accent. What amazed us even more was the completeness with which she had suppressed a whole side of her personality since marrying into the village perhaps seven or eight years previously. We must have met her dozens of times in the bright bareness of the village in winter, with no one else in sight, her head bowed, pushing her baby carriage, without picking up a hint of her American origins, as she nodded silently and passed. She was an earlier version of those, like Laura and the young flirtatious girls of the previous summer who had, perhaps casually at first, entangled themselves in the web of Italian village life. Now, it was as if she had entered an enclosed order, or taken a Moslem veil, so completely cut off had she become from people like ourselves. I do not know if the *bombardiere* forbade her, but apart from that one moment of openness, she never spoke to us again.

If these women were the unacknowledged legislators of the village, its acknowledged legislators were a second group of women. The village was run, consciously and unconsciously, by women, while the men hung around, procrastinated, got drunk and engaged in amateur dramatics. They were living, whether they admitted it or not, in a matriarchal order. There were fewer in this second category and it mostly comprised the women, married or single, who ran the *co-operativa*. They had had an idea, and they were fighting tooth and nail, against corporate male inertia and traditional prejudice, to put it into practice. Their leader, and the boss of the *co-operativa*, was a young woman called Michaela who had managed a shoe shop in Teramo before marrying a village man. Now, with a baby on one arm, she reckoned up the takings with the other, and delegated the tasks to her associates. She was bright and cheerful, but as tough as she had to be in facing down the reactionary backlash, from the Poggio commune as well as from inside the village itself.

But the women we had most in common with came from outside the village altogether. Such as Susanna, whom we had talked with over the kitchen table the previous autumn, before she had returned to teach in Teramo. In the spring she came back up again, to read Goethe, to breathe a little apart from her husband and children, and to go with her mother in search of wild asparagus in the woods. It was the season when the women slipped off to their secret haunts and returned with bundles of blackheaded stalks, their arms covered in cuts and scratches. The asparagus was only the first of many wild plants that would bring people into the mountains, in discreet competition, to pick them. Later there would be wild strawberries, wild mushrooms. For a while, Susanna told us, she was able to forget marriage and family, and to discover again something of her childhood.

Then there was Franca, the wife of Cesare. She used to say to us laughingly that we were a model couple, always together. What she meant was that she never saw her own husband, and apart from him she had only her two tiny children to talk to. Recently, besides his office job and his work for the commune, Cesare had taken another job gardening in the village in the afternoons, and he was less available than ever. After a winter of isolation, Franca was waiting for the one period in the year she looked forward to – her move north, for one of the summer months, to her family home in Turin.

'If I left altogether,' she said in her darker moments, 'I could make my living as a waitress.'

We were often the embarrassed witnesses of furious quarrels between the two of them – usually at their house, where we had been invited to eat. They both turned passionately to us as adjudicators – Cesare to me, Franca to my wife – and we struggled to extricate ourselves with a noncommittal comment. I think Cesare was rather glad our time in the village was coming to a close. We represented, in his mind, a possibility his wife had latched on to like a wish fulfilment. He suspected we had been putting ideas in her head. But our being there or not wasn't going to matter in the long run – he had brought into the village a wife too mentally sophisticated, a reader and thinker with no one to talk to but himself, and he was reaping the whirlwind.

Three weeks had passed since Alessandra's departure for Rome. Suddenly word came that she was home, though in bed, and available therefore only to the society of women. Stefania and my wife went over to see her, and found her in a huge double bed with a colour television for company. The operation had been successful, as had the first dose of chemotherapy. The prognosis was good. She was happy to be back in the mountains, but she was enjoying the luxury of feeling sorry for herself – she expected to be humoured. She might have lost a breast, but she had lost none of her old priorities.

'And you,' she started at both of them, 'when on earth are you going to have children?'

A few days later, we went over together for a much more cheerful meal than the last one. The old woman sat by the fire, drawing off the blacker energies into herself, while the noise level among the rest rose to its usual histrionic level. With the windows open at last and May outside, it was a good moment to come back to life. The living room was full of flowers, and an enormously sentimental card hung inside the front door. All this Alessandra professed to ignore, while secretly gloating over it. Things were back to normal.

Assured once more of life and femininity, she became her old, capricious self. At intervals she disappeared to Rome for treatments, but in between she cut a dramatic figure in the village, visiting her women friends and playing them off against each other. She knew she would never be coming back to work here, but would be transferred down the valley to a different village. So she behaved outrageously towards the villagers with whom, for the past nine years as postmistress, she had played cat and mouse.

In those days, because she was so free, we often drove out with her to visit old sites of pilgrimage in the mountains, or to gather wild flowers. She was a child, released into an endless summer. Not even the prospect of her daughter, distracted by the domestic crisis, having to repeat a year in school bothered her. It was all just blind life, it would work out. Of all the women we knew in and out of the village, she was the least conditioned either by necessity or intellect. She seemed to be governed by emotion alone. Now it was spring, and her life had been given back to her. We would not be around to see whether the spring, in fact, turned out to be an Indian summer.

22 WE WATCHED THE SHEEP being trucked back up the mountains. They had the same long-suffering air they had had the previous autumn. Their eyeballs peered through the wooden slats at us, in the pause while the lorries changed gear for the stretch of road above the village. By now, the snow had cleared in all but a few pockets of the upper valleys, and the green of Monte Gorzano above its treeline away to the north gave promise of good grazing. The return of the sheep marked the final transition in the mountains from spring to summer.

The May air was thick with drifting spores. Masses of them floated weightlessly through the hot, clear space between the trees. We breathed them into our nostrils and the backs of our throats and sneezed incessantly. In this greenhouse of accelerated growth, everything emerged all at once. Mushrooms with golden heads sprang out of cowpats, huge stonecoloured moths the size of our hands flitted about like bats at dusk, the horse in the corral by the bridge lay down and gave birth to a foal. After the months of stillness, it was like watching a film that someone slightly but significantly has speeded up.

It was still a film from which, by and large, human beings were absent. One by one the older people were drifting back up from the valley floor, but the hot square was still empty in the mornings and there was little traffic on the mountain road to Poggio. We seemed to be contemplating pure time, in which the non-human, the asocial, like understudies in the absence of the leading actor, crowded themselves into the centre of our attention. In May, that meant the flowers.

First, there had been the violets. Then a yellow carpet of primroses like footlights through the forest floor and, in the sheltered places at the base of treetrunks, the groups of wild cyclamens. In late April and early May, when these were starting to wane, the main consort erupted out of the dry soil of the Abruzzo and the crevices in its collapsing rock-faces. Suddenly, as if some *genius loci* in the middle of the mountains were releasing dyestuff, there were reds, blues and yellows everywhere – the papery petals of bloody cranesbills, the wild yellow ginestra celebrated by the dying Leopardi, the blue of cornflowers and harebells blowing in the tall grasses by the roadside. In the ditches were the brilliant miniatures of forget-me-nots and the white trumpets of bindweed. In the fields, neck and neck with the high grasses, the isolate bloodstains of poppies. As May gave way to June, the drugged sweetness of jasmine and honeysuckle thickened the evening air.

Among all this were the orchids, the pride of the Abruzzo, balanced on their slender green stems. Yellow orchids, mottled blue and white orchids, orchids of bright and dark pink, and the rare solitary bee orchids, their petals weirdly imitative of the back of a bee, for real bees to alight on and transfer their seed. Our eyes honed by months in the mountains, we picked them out in the grass.

Occasionally, in this botanical greenhouse, we met a local man we knew who had been out fishing in the deep pools in the declivities through which the stream roared. He warned us about snakes, but we only ever saw one, a small green one oozing up a crack in the rocks. He was fully rigged out with an angler's cloth bag and one of the long bamboo rods we had seen forests of, dapping in Italian rivers on Sunday afternoons. With this mighty rod the best he could hope to catch here were the tiny trout with which the Apennine streams were restocked each year, but it didn't seem to deter his enthusiasm. Italian sportsmen were aficionados of small game, be they trout or finches. Surprisingly, he ignored the most obvious trout of all, the three that swam, in season and out, in the green sunlit waters of the bridge pool, in full view of everyone.

All over Italy, in this quiet interim month, it was the time of pilgrimages. The priest announced the annual outing for the old people of the two villages, a pilgrimage to Fiesole, near Florence. It would leave at three thirty in the morning and return late at night. In the small hours of a May morning, twenty-four old people struggled along to the bridge to meet the bus coming down from Poggio. Late that night, when we were already half asleep, we heard the bus pulling up in the darkness of the square, and a tremendous racket of revivified old people shouting goodbye to each other and to their Poggio brethren. The following day Stefania, who to the derision of her friend Alessandra had gone along, told of a mighty day's feasting, drinking and singing. For many of the old people, it was the only day in the year they had been outside the village. For one or two, to judge by appearances, it was the last time they would ever leave it.

The season of the flowers came to an end. Scorched by the sun of early June, they began to lose their bloom and fragrance. There were still some, like the wild roses, whose season was ahead of them, but of the rest, only the tougher varieties, the cornflowers and yellow snapdragons, would survive the heat of July and August. The rest were gathered by Stefania, and on the still, hot morning of Corpus Christi, with her bucketfuls of yellow, blue and red petals, she formed religious images on the ground of the piazza, where they stayed just long enough to be seen by the procession the priest led through the village, before the hot wind of early afternoon made nothing of them forever.

In those last weeks of quiet, before the summer influx from America, a North African salesman appeared. So unexpectedly had he materialized, in his burnoose and coloured skullcap, that he might have dropped out of the sky. In reality, he must have taken a bus as far as he could into the mountains and hitchhiked the rest of the way, but he had the air of a man who had strayed off a medieval trade route eight hundred years ago, and had been wandering around up here ever since.

Not that his wares were medieval. Besides some strips of exotic carpet on his arm, he had a suitcase, which, without our asking, he opened. It contained cutlery, a few mirrors, and a large number of watches and clocks – as if time mattered to the people living up here. He didn't insist when we declined to buy, but folded away his wares with the same slow, deliberate air he had opened them, like a man used to getting little return for his effort, or none at all. He had come up from the south, he had desert experience.

After he left, I remembered others like him we had seen on the streets of Perugia and Bologna – vendors of watches and bootleg music, stamping their feet to stay warm, chatting to each other. Always the men, never the women, who stayed out of sight or had not yet come over from Africa. On the trains travelling north, we heard their guttural speech, like an endless clearing of the throat, so different from the Italian labials. They were illegal immigrants. There were so many of them that the Italian government had declared an amnesty for those who came clean within six months and acquired their working papers. Instead of resolving the problem, this had worsened it. They had wired their relatives and friends to come over while the going was good, and the numbers had swollen to three times their former size. Now, instead of clandestine illegality, there were mobs of Africans outside the *Quaestura* offices, clamouring for jobs and papers, while a racist backlash incubated itself in the local society.

All this had little to do with the village. It was a problem for the major cities, for Rome, Milan, Turin. We read about it in yellowed newspapers three days old – the riots against Africans in Florence, the police crackdowns, the deportations. It was a problem for Italy, and Italy, that mythical bureaucratic entity that existed only on paper, was somewhere else. Nonetheless, while untouched by the problem, our village philosophers had a point of view on it. Africa was for the Africans, Italy for the Italians. But the Italians, like the rest of Europe, had stopped producing children, while the Africans had not. Therefore, by laws of nature and survival, the extra numbers were migrating into the childless vacuums of Italy and elsewhere, to work on fishing boats and building sites, to wash floors and wipe windscreens, to do the dirty work that Italy felt it had risen above.

'We should treat these people with respect,' Renato had said to us one day. 'Not so long ago, we were in their position – immigrants, in Germany and America, doing other people's dirty work for them. Have we forgotten already?'

For an hour or two the North African salesman wandered around in the emptiness of the village, trying now this door, now that. We saw him through the window from time to time, with his heavy suitcase in one hand and his carpets in the other, and the increasing heat bearing down on him while he kept his air of ageless, stoical detachment. I don't think he sold anything, and after he had gone I felt that someone like him had probably always come through these villages, since the Middle Ages, but that now he represented something different, a threat perhaps. He was the forerunner of a newer, more massive nomadic age.

All this time, morning and afternoon, we had been doing our own work. As we well knew, this was shortly to come to an end. Every week there were more children whose parents had let them off school early. There were more lorries roaring past, more workmen with cement on their clothes, drinking into the small hours. In June, the advance guard of returnees from America began to appear in the neighbouring villages and in ours. From our point of view, the village was about to lose its most precious quality – its mountain silence.

There was, by now, something soft and blue about the mornings and evenings that killed off the impulse towards mental work, that took away the clarity and coldness and sense of definition of the autumn, winter and early spring that had made it such an ideal background for our kind of work. Now, in the middle of the day, the sun beat down and put the mind to sleep. We were forced to realize again that we were in the south, where life, more often than not, is the life of the body.

The room where I worked at the end of the house was again drifted with motes of light dust. Flies multiplied in proportion to my own mental distractions and buzzed against the windowpane with the illogicality of things trying to get inside one moment and out the next. By late May, I was well on the way to giving up whatever was on the inside and yielding completely to externality. I couldn't complain. What was wrong with the things I wrote was what was wrong with me. I was probably the only person in the village who could not blame his limitations on his surrounding environment.

I daydreamed, with the mountains in the distance. A large bumblebee struggled over the top of the worm-eaten windowframe and began to dunt against the mysterious element that separated it from its own world. In my case consciousness, in its case glass. I decided to lend it a helping hand.

The bee can't get out.
What will I do to help it?

Kill it, if I'm lazy.
If not, find a matchbox,

Trap it, for a moment,
And let it out the front door

To get its teeth into spring
The way I cannot.

My mental furniture was stacked away. The house, as far as I was concerned, was open to all comers. With the cessation of our mental work, we no longer had a real reason for being in the village, and its static atmosphere, instead of being an aid to concentration, became something we were restless to get away from into the flux of the big world again. The room where I had let my mind wander for a year reverted to itself again, a storehouse of inanimate objects, with a white dove perched on the sill, angled sunlight creeping over the floor, and the faint buzz of human conversation drifting up from below. As I closed the door on it for the last time, I thought how only now, when I was deserting it, had it come to embody what I had wished for my own mind all along – an ideal of pure emptiness, pure receptivity.

23 WITH CESARE, WE WENT back to the high passes. Since May, they had become accessible again, though still drifted with snow in the parts untouched by the arc of the sun's passage between the peaks. We were so high up, so ringed around with peaks, that to see them at all meant footing it a kilometre or so outside the village and changing our angle of vision. They were still there, lost in their own dark weather, as if belonging on another planet.

We were in no hurry to climb into the region of the peaks, and neither was anyone else in the village. They gave the impression that the heights meant nothing to them. In Poggio there was a mountain pride, but not here, where the terraced slopes the village was built on, apart from green patches of pasture for a few horses, had been abandoned by emigrant owners. None of this interfered with the wild natural beauty of the place, but what for us was aesthetic was for the village the lineaments of necessity. These were the conditions they had been born into. If they merited any comment at all, it was a curse. This was provided, loudly and publicly, by Gegeto when the weather came down.

We were moving into summer, but there were still days when the mists came down and hung weightlessly in the valley, and it was cold enough to feel glad of the stove. Although the plants were out, and the wild strawberries of early summer were there for the picking, it was still too cold for fireflies. In this uncertain weather, half glorious, half melancholy, we waited for Cesare to make up his mind about the peaks.

He knew a place, at a height of about six thousand feet under the peaks, where wild spinach grew around this time of year. His interest in spinach was an extension of the village women's interest in wild asparagus, nuts, berries and herbs in the woods nearby, and the secret places they went to on the quiet, year in year out. As far as spinach was concerned, he didn't have much competition from other villagers who by this stage in the twentieth century were content with the packeted varieties they could buy at the *co-operativa*. The jealous guarding of secret places where wild things, admittedly delicious, could be picked was a throwback, in the folk memory of the village, to the scarcities of the war years. For Cesare, a modern intellectual, it was perhaps something of an affectation, at odds with the actual tendencies of the village in which he had so consciously located himself. As for us, it was a long way to go for some spinach, but as good a pretext as any for getting further into the mountains.

We set off early one morning in the middle of June, with the mists still clearing from the peaks and the promise of a few hours at least of bright weather up there. Franca had declined to join us on the hike – she was still footsore, she said, from the one the previous summer – but she laid on a picnic and flasks of hot tea. We drove up to Poggio through layers of brightening mist and left the car there. By the time we had walked through its alleys and out the back end to where the hike began, the sun had flooded through and the peaks were visible. It was easy to see where we were headed,

easier than it would be to get there. Cesare pointed it out –
a shadowy patch high above the treeline, just beneath the
snowline. It was a long way away. For the first few kilometres, we slogged wordlessly along a trail beaten to an iron
consistency since the passage of the Romans across the
mountains from L'Aquila. If they had come in anything like
the armour they were noted for I pitied them, for before
long, in the magnified light of a high, closed valley under a
blue sky, we were streaming with perspiration. Everything
on the wane down below was still shooting into bloom up
here, and the air was thick with the hay fever of a belated
spring. Men on mountain bikes clattered past us on their
way back to Poggio after checking their flocks.

We passed a monument to a man killed in an avalanche
in 1929. He had disappeared up there in November and his
body had been discovered when the snow melted the following spring. Behind a glass inset in the monument was a
photograph of the victim, placed there by his relatives. It
showed a young bourgeois in shirt and tie, with slicked back
hair, smiling into the camera from some dining room in
Teramo. Up here in the gloom of the mountain pines it was
set among, it looked tiny and lost, the face of a newly dead
soul wandering in the frozen wastes of eternity.

If we had continued on the trail, we would have crossed
the mountains into L'Aquila. But Cesare cut across the
stream, still swollen with melting snow in June, and we
legged it up the slopes of the Corno instead, through the
green gloom of perpetual forest, sinking knee-deep in dead
leafmould. By this stage, we were blinded by our own sweat
and unable to gauge, because of the forest, how high we
actually were. Cesare had outstripped us to the point of

being a tiny figure zigzagging among broken timbers way ahead. Occasionally, we broke into small meadows. While he quartered them for mushrooms and herbs which he stashed in his rucksack, we got our breath back. Shooing horses, poking about in the long grass, he was entirely lost in what he was doing, and took little notice of us.

In this condition of wordless intimacy, we broke through the treeline to the bare upper slopes of the Corno. The sun was full in our faces, but a cold breeze funnelled between the peaks and dried the sweat on our brows. We kept our eyes to the ground as we trudged along, past a few gnarled outlying trees growing through the ruins of cowherd shelters. In this dehumanized grandeur, wild flowers had taken root among the skulls of dead cattle. There were types of orchid we hadn't seen lower down, and deep blue gentians pressed like buttonholes into the ground, linking us to the ecosystem of the Alps further north. As we climbed lazily through this profusion, Cesare had already reached where we were going. Spinach, not flowers was his priority. He was a man at work, and he had a better idea than we did how much time we had up there.

It was one in the afternoon when we sat down to eat the picnic. By Italian standards it wasn't a big one – meat, hard-boiled eggs and bread, with hot sweet tea that coursed through our blood like nectar, bringing the sugar balance back to normal. We had been on other picnics where the entire works were brought along – the pasta dish, the meat dish, the wines, coffee and liqueurs. From them, one staggered away in a haze of plenitude, with nature wheeling crazily in the background as one struggled to keep one's feet.

But this was a functional one, intended to restore our sapped energies for the job in hand.

The place, which was cold already and in shadow, had the effect of silencing us all. We were sitting in a high dark grassy nook, among boulders that were the remnants of a landslide. A few yards away, impacted among the boulders, was the hard grey snow of the peaks, at its lower limit. A cold wind blew continually off the snow, and combed the grasses among which the wild spinach grew. Cesare had been poking around already before we arrived, and he told us he had found broken stems. Someone else had been up there already. He was in a hurry to get started, and the sheer discomfort of the place prompted us to follow his example, if only to keep our limbs warm.

He had a large rucksack which we had to fill before we left. There was plenty of spinach about, though our assiduity in finding it was considerably less than this, and in my case a red-green colour-blindness probably meant that a certain amount of what was eventually cooked was mountain grass. As a plant, it was light, and it took a lot to make an impression on the rucksack, but for over an hour, in the cold wind and the shadow, we kept our heads down and browsed among the boulders. If nothing else, it was an object lesson in how hard life had been for the people up here in former years.

While we rested, Cesare worked on. In a strange way, the place suited him. Where work was concerned, he had a single-mindedness that excluded people, something we had seen in the village when he rigged a neon light for the *co-operativa* or tended a potato patch. He was a worker, where the other village men were socializers. They were pacing themselves through life up there – he was forcing the pace. As he beat about in the windy grasses, oblivious to all but himself and his work, the place seemed the ultimate expression of his solitary insistence on bringing his wife and children to the village in the first place.

Above us, cloud masses billowed and broke against the peaks, and scudded away downwind. There was nothing up there but rock, scree, blotches of frozen snow. Occasionally, one of the ravens that haunted the high pass into L'Aquila floated above us in the blue, but its caw was snatched away in a blast of wind. We could see now why Cesare had been in a hurry – an hour and a half was as much as one could hope for up here. The skies, with their giant cloud-shadows moving over the mountains, were bringing mists that would blot us out in a short while. It was a desolate spot.

We were perched on the spine of Italy – wild, jagged, broken by the irregular vertebrae of the peaks. To the south lay the plain of Fucino, where we had visited Silone country. North was Monte Gorzano and the central chain of the Apennines, dispersing into the mildness of the Umbrian hills around Perugia, where we had gone the previous November. The blue haze in the distance, half sea, half sky, was the Adriatic. Between it and ourselves, the rolling green hills of coastal Abruzzo rose to villages we had spent time in at one season or another. Higher again were Poggio and the ski resort, and our own village tucked away invisibly beneath them. We were looking back, in peace and detachment, on a whole year of our lives.

Cesare came back with a mass of spinach in his arms, and stuffed it into the rucksack. As the first drops of cold rain spattered about us, we drank from the thermos flasks. He was contented with his day's work. He was small and handsome, with a face like a monk from a Giotto fresco. 'Angeletto', his wife used to call him ironically when instead of quarrelling, they were only pretending to. No one would have suspected from his beatific face that dark domestic tempests hovered around him. Coming out here, although not a word had been exchanged on the subject, he had shown us his side of the story – work, theory, a necessary solitude.

At about half past two, in the middle of June, we left that pocket of wintry desolation. Going down was no easier than coming up. Despite his stuffed rucksack, Cesare was way ahead of us in no time, beating about among the grasses for whatever else he could find that was edible. With jellied knees, we wobbled after him into a blast of sunshine as we emerged from the shadow of the peaks. With his inner programme completed, he was more cheerful and in less of a hurry.

A grey drizzle had already obliterated the place where we had been. We sloshed across watery meadows full of lilies and rushes, where groups of horses drank. Sometimes we had the sound of water beside us, where sources foamed out of the porous, grassy rock, but more often an eerie silence. The upper slopes were waterless, broken here and there by patches of green where sheep browsed, tiny as animalcules. It was the absence of water that created the eerie silence – the absence of water, and the presence of cold, as the mountain chain looped north, from peak to peak, like something lunar, inhuman, that had nothing to do with Italy.

Cesare decided that instead of descending through the

trees, the way we had come up, we would walk directly down the shoulder of the mountain to our own village hidden beneath it. So we followed the treeline for a couple of kilometres to where it crested the shoulder, and then we plunged into the forest itself, a tangle of muddy paths, stepping-stones over oozy streams and branches that had to be scrambled through. Six hours after we had set off, our feet were doing the thinking for us. We would have crashed through a brick wall if they had told us to. As for the car, Cesare would get a lift up to Poggio later and collect it.

We emerged on to a series of tablelands cut like giant steps into the side of the mountain, dropping six feet at a time to the next level. At every level horses browsed, the sad-looking horses of the village put out to summer pasture, their rumps and underbellies scarred from whips and tightened straps. Herds of cattle tinkled about slowly, their crude metal cowbells around their necks. The superhuman dimensions of the steps led off into the blue space of afternoon, and we were on the edge of it. We felt tiny, as if a race of giants had preceded us.

We had been descending for the past two hours. We sat down and shared what was left in the thermos, and Cesare went in search of wild mushrooms. There were big white fungoid growths everywhere, but only a few edible ones – other villagers had come up on the quiet and beaten him to it. As he picked and discarded, lost in himself, I thought of Michele in Moravia's *La Ciociara*, the abstract idealist who goes against the grain of the mountain life he has been forced into along with other refugees from Rome, during the last war. That novel, set in the mountains a few hours east of where we were, tells of maladapted city people in their hundreds, scouring the high mountain terraces like these for herbs and berries, while the battle for central Italy rages on the coastal plains. Now, a whole decade had passed and there was only Cesare, escaped from the wars with his family, a solitary picker on terraces worked to death long ago by an emigrant people. And idealists were no more welcome in the village now than then.

When we got back to it, the village was asleep in silence and heat. It was six in the evening, and we had been nine hours on the mountain. Scrupulously, Cesare divided the contents of the rucksack on the kitchen table and took his leave with his own share. We took off our mountain boots. A delicious coolness flooded up through our feet from the stone floor.

24

HARDLY HAD WE REDUCED the spinach to a boiling mass in the pot when Silvio announced himself, with a violent thumping on the front door. It was the dinner hour, an unusual time for anyone to be about in the village, but he had not been home. His eyes had a benevolent film on them. He had been drinking. He was looking for company.

'You are great people,' he said with expansive sentimentality, 'great people, to have lasted this long in the village.'

He sat himself down at the kitchen table. We put the spinach aside, and dinner became whisky and cigarettes. As he talked, smoked and drank he looked around with the curiosity of one revisiting scenes from his own past. Apart from that one uproarious evening in January, it had been years since he had set foot inside the house.

'When I was a child,' he said, 'I used to be an altar boy for a ferocious priest who lived here. Then I left the church, like everybody else. I went to work in Calabria, as a draughtsman. And something happened. Drugs. I got sent to prison and lost my job.'

He drank at the whisky as a calmative. He was in a sentimental, retrospective mood, his eyes welling with tears as the emotion waxed and waned. He was crossing a divide in coming to see us, and he had chosen a moment when no one was looking. It was possible to intuit, through the fakery

and bravado, an intelligent sensitive man communing fur-
tively with his unacknowledged self.

'They are stupid morons,' he burst out, 'the men of this
village. They don't believe in God. Anyone with a grain of
intelligence believes in the existence of God. Do you have a
copy of Leopardi here? I'd like to recite for you.'

We fetched him a paperback edition of Leopardi, and he
thumbed through it with some hesitancy. Then he looked
up quickly and sharply at us.

'You're not doing this just to make fun of me, are you?'
he asked. 'You're not setting up this situation for your own
reasons?'

When he was satisfied that we weren't, he began to read
from 'L'Infinito' – not a very long poem, but after a few
lines he gave up in tears and threw the book aside.

Sempre caro mi fu quest'ermo colle,
E questa siepe, che da tanta parte
Dell'ultimo orizzonte il guardo esclude.

It was a strange situation, like one of those conversations we
had been reading in Dostoyevsky novels all winter, between
the protagonists and their potential murderers where an
ineffable sweetness and lyric abandon balances on a knife
edge with homicidal menace.

'You know who I am, don't you,' he suddenly said,
changing his tone and laughing nastily. 'You know my
reputation around here? You know my real business, don't
you? But if you were to spread it around outside this village,
it would be very, very unpleasant for you, d'you hear?'

He was enjoying his moment of power, the sense he was

projecting, as much to himself as to us, of a massively evil presence. But like the lyric interlude that preceded it, this too passed away in a flash. He was too drunk to present anything of a threat, but his eyes, his infinitely intelligent and sensitive eyes, looked out at us from the goldfish bowl of solipsistic suffering he was swimming around in, without hope of communication. We would never understand each other – we were the outsiders, he the complete insider. The language of his private suffering, and that of the village in general, was a closed book to us.

'You have intelligent eyes,' he said to us both, after a brief pause.

Instead of using the word '*intelligente*' he used the word '*furbo*' which, besides intelligence, has overtones of cuteness, craftiness. Momentarily, it made us feel uncomfortable again, almost guilty, as if we owed him some further explanation for our presence in the village. All year this sophisticated man, a mixture of intelligence and drunken pathos, had been taking the measure of us. He still couldn't quite make up his mind whether he liked us or despised us, but he was giving us the benefit of the doubt.

'You are great people,' he said again, as he embraced us and took his leave. 'Great people to have stayed in the village.'

When he had gone, we went back to the spinach – Cesare and his innocent idealism! But in the small hours of the morning, when the village was dark and silent again, we were woken by an even more violent pounding on the front door. It was Silvio, shouting drunkenly that he wanted to continue the conversation, it interested him. This time, as we could hear, he had brought his friends. As the shouting and pounding continued, we were seized by a kind of apprehension we had not known since the house had been stoned by teenagers the previous autumn – the sense of being isolated, outside the law and completely vulnerable. We lay in the dark and listened, until, with a final kick of frustration against the door, he roared with laughter and went away.

This, which was little enough in itself, was our last real event. From then on, the summer returnees flowed in like a tide, and we merged with them as we had the previous summer, like extras in a crowd scene. But it showed us how different things might have been, if, during the long months when we were alone up there, we had attracted the wrong sort of attention. Through unobtrusiveness, we had gotten by. It might easily have been otherwise. Apart from the changing of the seasons, and the liturgical calendar, our time up there was characterized by a lack of external happenings. It was life reduced to the domestic, the local and the natural, with the great dynamos of work and history removed. But the minutiae of life loomed larger. Whether someone said hello or didn't. The meaning of a passing glance, a nod, an expression. Without many words being exchanged, everyone had developed an almost marital intimacy with each other over the years, going beyond love or hate. Their world was bounded by a few houses, a bridge on either side of the village, and the provincial town of Teramo. Behind these, and providing the essential weather, both physical and psychic, of the place, were the mountains. Those who wanted something different had long since left.

In its own small way, it embodied certain truths about

Italy in general, about Europe even. It had been lost and abandoned by its own people, who had gone west, and now it was about to be rediscovered, with its physicality and its acute sense of limit, as not the worst way to have lived. Sometimes, living up there, I imagined all the deserted houses there must be all over Europe, all the other empty spaces we might have taken up residence in – places marked like this by the failure of a religious idea or its secular alternative, but where a certain stoicism prevailed, a scepticism better than nothing. The quietly maternal, like Laura, and the overtly idealistic, like Cesare, saw in it certain possibilities. It was a time when Europe, after a long period of negation, was having second thoughts about itself.

We had been lucky up there. It had been an unusually fine winter, a disaster for the mountain resorts but a considerable easing of our circumstances. So fine had it been that the watertable had gone unreplenished, and a drought was expected later that summer. Even before we had left, water rationing had begun in the village. Our taps went dry for an hour or two each afternoon.

We had been lucky, too, in the priest. His help had been critical, especially in the early days when there was no shop in the village, and later on in the winter when he brought us up the kerosene that kept the stove going. His greatness as a man, his extraordinary drive and appetite for work, was ill-matched to the slow, introverted temper of the village. A different kind of clerical greatness was required to get through to the soul of the place. But for that perhaps a different kind of belief altogether was needed than the one whose chapels and shrines, as we had seen, were grassgrown ruins through the Abruzzo mountains.

His greatest gift to us, though, was the house itself. Physically, it was crumbling beside the church it was attached to. Spiritually, it was the other way around. Its three thick walls and the dusty rooms they contained, its kitchen, hearth and upstairs rooms looking out on the mountains, its black stove with the crooked pipe beside which our books gathered a sooty fallout – all this became for us a place of inner, secular excitement while the ecclesiastical powers, so to speak, looked the other way. He never fully understood why two apparently intelligent people would want to winter in such a house. But to his credit he raised no objections, and when, the following summer, we closed the door on it for the last time, it was with the sense of having made it completely our own.

Now, when I remember the village, I remember blue stillness, contemplative time. I think I can see what everyone there is doing at any given time of the day. An illusion, of course. People have died and moved away. And the house itself is roofless, its inside being transformed into something else. We were the last to have lived there.

The evening before we left, we walked over to Prato to say goodbye to Alessandra. We had walked that stretch of road times without number, in all kinds of weather – fine autumn days, freezing winter dusks when the wind off the snow was painful to our ears, summer mornings when we met old women picking wild strawberries, tiny and sweet, from their private hideaways. We followed its wide loop down to the bridge and up the opposite side of the ravine to the headland. From there, we looked back at our own village.

Above us, the Plough was suspended as it had been the

night we arrived. In the course of the year, it had bumped like an old bedstead round the peaks until it came full circle. The dusk wind from the upper valleys that cools the mountains in summer brought us, ever so faintly, the sounds of our own village across the ravine, a little parcel of lights more intensely lurid around the bar, with cars coming and going to and from it, tiny and intermittent as the fireflies we had just seen in the woods. The coming into season again of the fireflies, and the completed round of the Plough above the peaks, the infinitesimal and the immense, marked the passage of our year.

It was a warm blue night that brought everyone out of their houses. Hormonal rage had seized the teenagers, who roared around the village on motorbikes, shedding a wake of sparks. The older people, feeling a superfluous vitality welling up in them, engaged in shouting matches. Where we sat in the grasses of the headland, there were love-cars with their lights turned down. We listened up there to the village, coming as a faint tintinnabulation on the breeze, before descending into Prato.

There was music in Prato, a rough male chorus repeating itself over and over like a football chant, coming from we knew not where. Not from the lit, crowded bar we passed on the way to Alessandra's, where her husband Stefano sat playing cards and the barmaid Alessandra had sourly described as '*molto provocativa*' was serving drinks. Not from the moonlit square in front of the church, where the old people sat out talking and minding the young children. But from somewhere nearby, one of the side streets, came the rhythmic chanting.

We knocked on the door of Alessandra's house, in its

quiet, leafy avenue. An upstairs window opened and her daughter leaned out, a girl of fourteen, her brown shoulders bare but for brassière straps, the nimbus of emergent sexuality in her loose, honey-coloured hair. Alessandra was in the village, she said, at the marriage celebrations. Did we not hear the chanting? She herself was still dressing, and would go there later. We said goodbye to her, and asked her to say goodbye to Alessandra if we did not see her up in town.

We followed the sound of the singing into the centre. Up a side street, a crowd of young men were in full voice in front of a darkened upstairs window. The bride was up there, one of them told us, and she would remain hidden. Tomorrow she would be married here in town, and then they would go away for a while. But, miracle of miracles, they had decided to come back and settle here in Prato. The singing drowned out his next words, the singing and the stamping of feet, and the occasional crash of a breaking bottle or glass. From a lit room on the ground floor, the bride's mother was serving wine to all comers through an open window. We took a glass each and raised it, in the warm night full of singing – to marriage, to the mountains, to the good thing our life there had been.